GOING BACK TO GO FORWARD

*identify the wounds,
release the pain,
step into healing*

GOING BACK TO GO FORWARD

*identify the wounds,
release the pain,
step into healing*

REBECCA COLEY

Going Back to Go Forward © 2025 by Rebecca Coley. All rights reserved.

Published by Greatness Makers
PO Box 213067, Columbia, SC 29221

www.GreatnessMakers.com

All rights reserved. This book contains material protected under international and federal copyright laws and treaties. Any unauthorized reprint or use of this material is prohibited. No part of this book may be reproduced or transmitted in any form or by any means, electronic or mechanical, including photocopying, recording, or by any information storage and retrieval system, without express written permission from the author.

Identifiers:
ISBN: 979-8-9943115-9-2 (paperback)
ISBN: 979-8-9943115-8-5 (hardback)
ISBN: 979-8-9943115-7-8 (ebook)

Available in paperback, hardback, and ebook

Unless otherwise stated, all scriptures are taken from the New American Standard Bible (NASB).

Scripture taken from the New King James Version®. Copyright © 1982 by Thomas Nelson. Used by permission. All rights reserved.

Scripture quotations marked TPT are from The Passion Translation®. Copyright © 2017, 2018, 2020 by Passion & Fire Ministries, Inc. Used by permission. All rights reserved.

Scripture quotations are taken from the Holy Bible, New Living Translation, copyright ©1996, 2004, 2015 by Tyndale House Foundation. Used by permission of Tyndale House Publishers, Carol Stream, Illinois 60188. All rights reserved.

Amplified — Scripture quotations marked AMP taken from the Amplified® Bible (AMP). Copyright © 2015 by The Lockman Foundation. Used by permission.

COPYRIGHT

Amplified Classic — Scripture quotations taken from the Amplified® Bible (AMP), Copyright © 1954, 1958, 1962, 1964, 1965, 1987 by The Lockman Foundation. Used by permission.

Any Internet addresses (websites, blogs, etc.) and telephone numbers printed in this book are offered as a resource. They are not intended in any way to be or imply an endorsement by Greatness Makers, nor does Greatness Makers vouch for the content of these sites and numbers for the life of this book.

Dedication

To my husband,

You are the one who stood in the storms with me, lifted my chin when I could barely lift my head, and loved me with a depth I didn't yet have for myself. You believed in the woman I was becoming long before I could see her, speaking courage over me in whispers and in strength.

You held my heart when it was fragile, cheered for me when my voice was shaking, and supported me with a faithfulness that carried me through every chapter of healing. God used your steady love to remind me that I was worth fighting for.

Thank you for choosing me and seeing me.

Contents

Foreword	XI
Acknowledgements	XIII
A Father's Blessing	XV
Introduction	1
1. Growing Up	7
2. Meeting Jesus	23
3. Spiritual Mothers and Sisters	27
4. Divorce and Church Hurt	29
5. Cultivating a God Time	34
6. Journaling the Voice of God	45
7. 44	76
8. Jehovah Rapha	82
9. Going Back to Go Forward	96
10. Healing vs Coping	101
11. Opening the Heart	113

12.	Forgiveness	123
13.	Judgments	138
14.	Processing Memories	145
15.	Emotions and Emotional Needs	152
16.	Rejection	174
17.	Lies	181
18.	Grieving	192
19.	Keep going	207
20.	The Place	215
About the Author		217

Foreword

REBECCA'S JOURNEY IS ONE where trauma did not win, Jesus did!

There comes a point in every believer's journey when we realize that salvation, while instantaneous, is only the beginning of God's work in us. The deeper healing of the heart, the kind that restores our peace, our identity, and our capacity to love, is a process that unfolds as we walk closely with Jesus. Rebecca's book is a companion for that sacred journey.

Within these pages, you will find truth that touches the hidden places, those wounded corners of the soul that we often keep tucked away. You will discover that God is not intimidated by our brokenness; He runs toward it. His desire is to make us whole, to turn our pain into purpose, and our scars into stories of grace.

Rebecca writes not as one untouched by life's hardships, but as someone who has walked through the valley and found Jesus faithfully there. Through Scripture, reflection, and testimony, her book invites you to lay down your burdens and let the Holy Spirit gently uncover what needs healing. It is an invitation to trust again, to forgive, to be free.

If you open your heart as you read, I believe you will encounter the tender presence of the One who "heals the brokenhearted and binds up their wounds" (Psalm 147:3). May her words lead you closer to the Healer Himself, Jesus and may you emerge with a deeper awareness of His love, stronger than every wound, and greater than every fear.

— Pastor Denise Boggs
  Founder of Living Waters Ministry

The vision God gave Pastors Lee and Denise for Living Waters ministry was much over 30 years ago and is being fulfilled and continues to unfold. This ministry has become an international ministry touching thousands of lives around the world.

Acknowledgements

Papa Ken,

Thank you for teaching me how to truly connect with God and hear His voice for myself. Your "yes" to Jesus not only transformed your life, but it forever changed mine. The investment you and Linda made in my walk with God continues to bear fruit in every life this message reaches. Thank you for seeing me, hearing my heart, and believing in what God placed within me. I am deeply grateful to God for the gift you both are to my heart and my life.

Ken and Linda Helser are the founders of A Place for the Heart. Founded in 1986, God spoke to them to create a safe place where people could come away from the busyness of life and encounter God's heart. This ministry continues to thrive and touch the world through discipleship schools and ministry of song through their son and daughter-n-law, Jonathan and Melissa Helser.

Erin,

I am so thankful for you designing the cover of this book. Thank you for truly hearing my heart and seeking the Holy Spirit throughout this process. You asked the right questions and helped bring God's vision for this book to life with excellence and care. Thank you for honoring me and for your beautiful creativity. I am deeply grateful for you and your gift.

Erin Gravitt is a mixed media artist from Asheboro, NC specializing in watercolor painting. With Indonesian heritage, Erin loves bringing beauty to life through bright colors and patterns. As a mother of three, Erin's art brings beauty into the mundane with bold and decisive colors. In addition to her own creative work, Erin serves as an art teacher with the Cageless Birds community in Sophia, NC.

A Father's Blessing

C S Lewis wrote: "God whispers to us in our pleasures, but shouts to us in our pain. Pain is God's megaphone to draw our attention to Him".

When Rebecca had tried everything but Jesus because of her own painful wounds that created havoc in her body, God's megaphone of pain drew her to Jesus, and she chose the narrow road that Jesus said, "This road is the road to life, the road that brings healing and health, but few men would take this road, instead they wander on the easy and wide road that leads to death".

When my wife and I met Rebecca at the entrance of a wholesale store, she introduced herself to us with smiles of exclamation, "My goodness, it's Ken and Linda from A place for the Heart. Oh how I have prayed for you guys and I love you so much. You are always in my intercession, but now I get to see you face to face. Oh how much I love you and your ministry. You are always in my heart." What an introduction. And with that we sought out a relationship with her and her husband, Tim. We often met at our daughter's place for a meal or coffee, but mostly for fellowship. And little did I know that traumatic healing was taking place in Rebecca's life, until I read her book. That's because she was always so full of joy and hope she never showed the pain she was walking through. Oh what a journey of recovery she traveled on for years, then she took the time as busy as she was reaching out to others with healing words and counsel, but she took the time to record both her journey and how the Lord enabled her to overcome the deep wounds of rejection through forgiveness, healing of memories, through walking back into her painful past with the healer Himself, Jesus! Yay God!

As I was reading along engulfed in story how the Lord first diagnosed the painful source that was the root cause of her many painful sicknesses in her body, she would suddenly stop, and there was this strange word: "PROMPT" In other words her book was not just a story as amazing as it was, but she took the time like the Good Samaritan to help me, you, the reader to take a cup of refreshment and healing from the Good Shepherd that met her needs and that He would do the same for us. So, I quickly got what "Going Back to Go Forward" was all about.

The essence of the reason God impressed Rebecca to write was so that He could reach others in the same way He met her. As I read Rebecca's heart steps with her Healer Jesus, my mind kept recalling the many years I ministered at Women's Prison in Raleigh. Eight years of monthly Thursday evenings with so many wounded lives, and I thought how much her book could bring freedom to each inmate.

If only I could have placed "Going Back to Go Forward" into the hands of the 963 inmates that were all in prison because they lived out lives distorted from the very pain Rebecca was healed from. And what really ministered to me is that she gained so much wisdom and tools on how to process the rejection, the abuse, the pain, the forgiveness, the healing of memories and on and on, and she shared these healthy and productive tools through giving her brokenness to Jesus, and in turn how He used her openness to Him. She shared with everyone who reads this book the hope to get well!

— Ken Helser
Founder of *A Place for the Heart*

Ken and Linda Helser are the founders of A Place for the Heart. This ministry is located on 52 acres of land in Sophia, North Carolina. Founded in 1986, God spoke to them to create a safe place where people could come away from the busyness of life and encounter God's heart. This ministry continues to thrive and touch the world through discipleship schools and ministry of song through their son and daughter-n-law, Jonathan and Melissa Helser.

> Rebecca,
> So glad He brought you through each painful episode in your life, because now others can learn the ways of God to get well themselves! So helpful. I gained so much from reading the entire book. I've been helped by your words and more than ever can't wait to purchase many to pass onto those suffering from what you were healed from. Yay God!
> Love you and Tim big!

Introduction

WHEN SHARING PIECES OF my story, people would respond with comments like, "You should write a book." I would just nod and smile at them, thinking, "Maybe someday."

I started hearing that phrase from more people, and the idea of actually writing a book began to stir in my heart. Sometime later, someone said to me, "So *when* are you going to write that book?"

I knew then it was time.

So here it is! Words that contain my story. A story of deep wounding, but one where the healing power of Jesus touched, covered, and healed. I'm not a victim of trauma but, truly, more than a conqueror in Christ Jesus.

Saying "yes" to Jesus for Him to come into my life (the Bible calls it being reborn) gave me new life and a new perspective. In that new life, I also received an invitation to welcome Jesus into every painful place for Him to touch. Accepting Jesus didn't mean the wounding I had experienced was instantly healed, though some of it was. It meant receiving a Helper to do just that—help me through painful places. Places that would be touched and reframed by His kindness. He would heal my heart and rewrite my story. He would tenderly touch the places of hurt and anger in such a kind way that my soul would surrender and begin trusting Him in a deeper capacity.

I will share my story and what I've learned over the years that has brought peace and healing to my heart and soul. This book is real, a testimony of my life with God. The journey of going back to go forward. Practices, disciplines, and choices that God used to help my heart heal from deep wounding and pain.

Throughout this book, when I use the term "God," I am referring to God the Father, God the Son Jesus, and God the Holy Spirit.

We have all been through hard and painful things, and we will continue to experience them. In life, sometimes the painful things that have happened are compounded by hurts that originated years, sometimes decades, before. In my case—and in the lives of many that I have ministered to—the existing pain was stuffed down in our hearts without being processed because we didn't know how to process, or we think coping is healing.

So, in our current day-to-day life, when painful situations or loss happen, it can shake us to our core. If we have tools, we can process what's happened in our pasts, bringing healing to the hurts in such a way that even the memory no longer holds the power to shake us. Then when new painful situations occur, they're no longer being compounded by the wounds from our pasts, allowing us to process them. Neither difficult circumstances, trauma, abuse, loss, nor anything that hurts our hearts needs to mark or define us, but can be marked and defined by the healing power of Jesus. If we welcome Jesus into the painful parts, He can and will rewrite our stories to bring healing and peace to any situation.

My life feels like one big processing story, but healing is a journey not a destination. Today, I'm not where I was last month, last year, or ten years ago. I'm stronger, steadied in my heart, and my vision has been touched by heaven. I know where I have been and where I am going. My hope is that in sharing my heart and life, someone might gain hope, courage, and confidence that their story matters and see the importance of healing. I have truly experienced the unfathomable love, healing, compassion, mercy, and grace of God that's on the other side of pain and trauma. My passion is for others to experience the same.

One of my favorite scriptures is Psalms 23:6a in The Message translation (MSG) that says, "Your beauty and love chase after me every day of my life." God's word is truth. His beauty and His love have chased me every single day of my life.

My story is the forever testimony of how God's loving kindness chased and caught me. He has been faithful to me even when I wasn't faithful to Him. I have learned His love and faithfulness aren't dependent on how good I am, but are based on His character, His love, and His mercy. Knowing God's character and His love makes us want to serve Him with all our hearts.

The first "service" we are called to is intimacy with Him. It's not preaching the Gospel, serving in our church, or going on mission trips, though all of that is good. The first service is knowing

Him, because knowing Him is where life is found. In that secret place—as the Bible refers to it in Psalms 91—is where He reveals His love, compassion and kindness to us. It was in that space that I felt like an orphan who became a daughter. His goodness began washing over my heart, rejuvenating places where the pain cried out and demanded to be heard. And in that place, when God heard the cry of my pain, He moved in closer.

Now, if I sat and shared my full story in detail with you, the traumas, abuse, and the sin, you might question those words. You might even ask, "Was God really good?" Isn't that the temptation from all the way back in the Garden of Eden, to question if God is truly good? I can tell you, even in the darkest mess and deepest pain, trauma, and sin, God was and still is good. The situation might not be good, but He will work it out for our good.

> You intended to harm me, but God intended it all for good.
> —Genesis 50:20 (NLT)

God wants to bring healing to our hearts. When He sent someone that said God wanted to heal *my* heart, I kind of scoffed inside because I didn't think I needed any more healing. But their words touched something, and I could feel God calling me deeper. The scoffing? Well, that was pride, and He would address that too—He told me so.

The pain was dark, but God was the Light.

As I said before, healing our hearts is a journey, not a destination. It's a process. Giving voice to the pain that was buried in silence started the process of receiving God's peace and healing. Situations didn't change, but I changed.

The trauma, abuse, sin, hurt, disappointments, and rejection in my life are pieces of where the enemy tried to destroy me, but where Jesus remained with me, and His kindness wrapped around me. In Jesus is where healing and safety was and is. His tender love touched and is touching, healed and is healing, all the brokenness and pain.

Jesus truly was and still is my safe place. He not only wants to be that for me, but He desires to be that for you. He has tenderly guided me, never leaving my side; even when my choices separated me from fellowship with Him, He was still there. He has been patient with me, my heart, and my decisions. Jesus sought me to bring healing to every facet of my being, and I said "yes" to His pursuit of my heart. He came.

I welcome you into my story.

Chapter One
Growing Up

There was pain but there would come healing.

To share my story, we need to go back to my childhood so you can receive insight and understanding of what God wanted to heal. I'll break it down into segments and will share processes that helped my heart heal. The healing power and the longing of God's heart to heal us is very real.

Childhood

The wounds wouldn't fade but would be healed.

My childhood was split between two places, my mom's house with her and my stepfather, and at my maternal grandparents', whom I affectionately call Nana and Pawpaw. My biological father was not in my life when I was a child. When I was with Nana and Pawpaw, life felt easier, simpler. I could be a child, run and play and laugh. I felt no sense of danger. They were very poor, but their love for me was rich. Nana would look at me with a soft smile, the creases of her thin lips filled with snuff.

If you don't know what snuff is, it's a powdery tobacco product. And in my opinion, it's awful! It even smelled awful. If the wind moved even slightly as she was spooning it into her mouth, the scent seemed to travel everywhere.

Pawpaw was a tall man at over 6', from what I remember. His hands were larger than life and reached out tenderly to me. I heard stories of how they weren't always tender and that he was a man with deep and terrible anger, though I never witnessed that. I remember playing hide and seek with him and taking trips to get hot dogs. On one of those trips, he purchased a floral Hawaiian bandana—I must have been around seven years old—and it was a big deal to me. I loved the colors, and I still have that bandana. As a little girl, I always felt safe around him, like no one could or would hurt me. He would protect me. He was my safety.

I first heard of Jesus from Nana, and she often took me to church with her. When in their home, I remember seeing preachers on the small black and white T.V. She watched them intently, as if they were speaking directly to her soul, and sometimes, she would receive mail from them. But the one thing that sticks out more than anything is that she taught me to pray. Every night I stayed with her, we would lie in bed, and she had me visualize the neighbors, praying over each house I saw. Then we would progress to praying out loud the name of each aunt, uncle, and cousin. I believe that is where God taught me to see spiritually. As I prayed and called out their names, I saw their faces, and this would continue until I fell asleep next to my nana. In her arms, I felt very loved and safe.

Though a grandchild of many—I think there were around 18 grandchildren at that time—I always felt seen and loved. There were always oatmeal cookies hidden away in the kitchen for me. To this day, I still love those cookies. I enjoyed breakfast sitting on a stool with Nana on my right and Pawpaw on my left. I giggle now as I recall him eating oatmeal with so much sugar it was like syrup. There, at their table, I felt like I belonged, was accepted, was part of a family. It was as though there was space made just for me, a space where I was welcomed and invited to sit. To this day, breakfast (or breakfast foods) remains my favorite meal. I'm sure much of that is because of the fond memories linked to my heart.

Time and life at my mom and stepfathers' house were very different. What I'm about to share is not to put any shame or condemnation on my mom but to give you insight into my life. This is my story. Today, after much heart work and healing with Jesus, I can honor my mom by forgiving her and extending mercy and compassion. I realize her life was hard. I believe fear motivated many things she did and didn't do. Hurting people truly hurt people, sometimes intentionally and sometimes unintentionally. Life there was hard—hard for her. Growing up for her wasn't easy.

As you probably realize by now, there was a lot of dysfunctions, trauma, pain, confusion, rejection, fear and the like in my childhood. I had been exposed to more trauma than most adults would even hear of in a lifetime, through sexual, emotional, and physical abuse. The sexual abuse started before I even had memory of it at barely two years old. I only know that because, in my early 20s, I received a call from a relative. She shared the guilt she felt because she had walked in on a man abusing me when I was only a toddler. That man would continue abusing me for years.

When she began sharing the story of what she saw, things began to make sense. My body remembered, shaking from the trauma, and the memories began rushing to the surface of my heart. It felt as though I was carrying the injuries in my very soul. All the sexual, emotional, and physical abuse was still very real. The physical abuse called "spankings" caused fear from not being able to cry or else "getting something to really cry about." The bruises, shame, and embarrassment of the terrible things that had been done to me haunted me throughout my childhood, adolescent years, and into adulthood as I worked on healing lies like "children are to be seen and not heard," or "I brought you into this life and I can take you out of it."

This shook me to my core, and the fear that came in took residence in my little heart. The enemy has a way of watching what we are feeling and then planting a lie to match it. Or maybe he plants the lie and the feelings follow. Either way, the lies will get wrapped up in a feeling, making them seem like the truth. Lies that cripple you. Wounding that invites the kingdom of darkness to have access and bring destruction. Oh, but the Kingdom of Light was watching, and Jesus would come. He would save, heal, and deliver. I would not be left alone—not as a child nor as an adult.

At my first sleep over as a little girl, my friend didn't feel safe, so she faked a stomachache to go home. I was so embarrassed and confused, not realizing my home wasn't safe. I thought everyone's home was like mine. Later in adulthood, that would be a memory I processed with Jesus, to let Him heal and release the shame that lingered over my heart and in my soul. As a child, I did what I had to do, stuffing all the pain and hurt down deep and ignoring the troubled waters inside my heart. I learned how to stop feeling and to stop trusting. I learned to cope.

As an adult, I know my mom did the best she could, but I would still need to process some really difficult things to be able to release the pain, hurt, confusion, and the like. While the wounding of my heart and body was happening, the little girl that I was could not articulate that my mom's life was hard or comprehend what she may have endured. I formed what felt like just an opinion, but now I realize it was a very harsh judgment against her. I will talk more about this later.

Now, after processing some deep pain, I can see, accept, and have compassion for my mom. Her life was hard, and she had experienced many of the same things I had. For a long time, I made excuses for what happened because my mom's childhood and life were hard, and she experienced trauma too. But when we make excuses for others, we don't heal—we stuff down the pain instead of facing it. We don't honor our parents by making excuses. We do the opposite. The first way we honor is by forgiving their shortcomings, their sins, and releasing that to Jesus. That's how we gain peace, even in relationships where the other person hasn't changed.

Pain must be talked about and felt to be healed. In my childhood home, you didn't talk about what you were feeling. Whether you were sad, lonely, afraid, it didn't matter. You were not allowed to speak of it or speak about what was being done to you. Again, I just assumed everyone's home must be like this, that everyone must feel the way I did inside. Sometimes, though, every once in a while, I would feel like something was terribly wrong. Surely this wasn't normal. But I did what I had to do to cope. I stuffed down all the red flags and ignored the big things happening in my little heart.

As adults, to live emotionally healthy lives and mature spiritually, our hearts must have space to be heard. We must process what happened in our childhoods and give voice to the silent pain—especially from the ages of birth to 13 years old, as these years are most important. We need safe places to be seen and heard, where we can talk about what happened so our hearts can begin to heal and release the sin done to us.

As I shared before, even if we know or believe that our parent(s) did the best they could, or that they really didn't know what they were doing and so on, the child inside of us at the time didn't know that. The feelings of those painful events get buried, swept under the rug. Pain must be felt to be healed, so we must give voice to what happened for our hearts to heal.

We must go back that we may go forward. There would come a day, decades later, where that little girl who had become a woman would need to process the painful places. She would need to forgive and release. Let's talk about how I did just that.

Going Into Teenage Years

The wounds were deep, but God's love would be deeper.

When I was around nine years old, Pawpaw got very sick. I saw him in the hospital, the one who was bigger than life, as he laid still and fragile. He soon passed away. On the way to the graveside, I saw a dark-skinned man on the side of the road saluting us as we drove by. That honor that he gave a stranger set upon my heart. I remember his solemn face. It was as though he could see, even as the car passed by, the sadness I felt.

As I think about this memory now, I wonder about who that man was. I feel deep within that he was possibly an angel sent by God to capture what was happening in my little heart. The sadness seemed bigger than I was, and though we didn't talk about it, I could feel the heavy lingering. My nana's house felt different; she was different.

Death would have a domino effect, and many others in my life would begin passing away. Each year, a significant death took place, and I had no idea how to grieve losses. I don't think anyone around me truly did. In my 40s, God would reveal that Pawpaw had been my security, and I would need to grieve and process not only losing him, but the loss of my security and my father figure. I would then learn what grieving truly was and how to process losses, not just people, but dreams, expectations, and so on.

Around 11 years old, my stepfather passed away, and that brought a lot of change. My sister was only four years old, and we would bury her father on her fifth birthday. At that time, we lived in a mobile home beside his mother. We abruptly had to move our mobile home, and life became confusing. Mom didn't have the funds and had two little girls to care for. The shock and confusion lay over our hearts like a cold blanket that smothered instead of comforted.

I knew I should pray to God, but wondered where He was. My mom was hurting. I picked up all her pieces and did my best to take care of her and my sister before my uncle took them in. Not sure when, why, or how it was decided, but I went to live with Nana. Her home had always been a safe haven before, and though I was the same, it felt different somehow. It was as though the spark of joy had been replaced with pain, hurt, and confusion.

By the age of 13, it felt like I was drowning, that the darkness was swallowing me. By this point, my mom was able to have the mobile home moved beside my Nana, and we were all back there together. But so were other men. It still not in a place of safety. The pain inside my heart could no longer be ignored, and I struggled with such anger against my mom. I blamed her for all that had been done to me, holding her fully responsible. Feelings buried alive don't die. They eventually emerge, either in a healthy manner by processing them, in anger, or sometimes sideways in sickness. I wouldn't deal with the sickness piece until a few decades later.

So, as a 13-year-old girl, I sat on the bank in front of our mobile home as all the pain that I had been burying, all the rejection, all the sadness, everything came rushing to the surface of my heart and mind. It was more than my heart could handle. It seemed as though every demon that had been given access to my soul through the wounding I experienced had full access, and in that moment, I had a very real conversion with God. I said, "God, I have heard that all children go to heaven. I'm 13 now, so I don't know if I'm a child or adult. I don't know if You'll let me in heaven or not. If You won't let me in heaven, I'd rather die and go to hell than live like this anymore."

I believed I didn't have the capacity to feel all the pain I was feeling anymore. I stood up, took a deep breath, and made the decision to end my life. I walked inside the mobile home and looked for pill bottles. My stepfather had been very sick, so there was plenty of medication that was easily accessible. If the pills were small enough that I could swallow, I consumed them, literally bottles upon bottles.

My mom came home shortly after I swallowed the pills. When she found me, she immediately called 911 and emergency services came. I have minimal recollection, but I was told my blood pressure dropped into single digits and that I died three times on the way to the hospital. I woke up days later from a coma with my nana's pastor praying over me. Prayer is powerful! God was not going to let my life be taken by darkness and pain. His plans were good. Satan's plans were evil.

> The thief comes only in order to steal and kill and destroy. I came that they may have *and* enjoy life, and have it in abundance [to the full, till it overflows]. I am the Good Shepherd. The Good Shepherd lays down His [own] life for the sheep.
>
> —John 10:10-11 (AMP)

> For I know the thoughts that I think toward you, says the Lord, thoughts of peace and not of evil, to give you a future and a hope.
>
> —Jeremiah 29:11 (NKJV)

I eventually went home from the hospital, and while nothing had changed, *everything* had changed. I still couldn't cope with what was inside of me, so much rage, pain, and confusion. I tried so hard to push it down, to just forget it, but bad things were still happening—things too terrible for me to even share. I thought things would change, but I was still in a hard place. I developed eating disorders that plagued me. I was about 5'6" and maybe 90-95 pounds. The one thing I could control was my food, so I controlled that one part of my life.

As I said before, pain that is buried doesn't just go away. It remains. Eventually, it must be felt and dealt with to be healed.

As a frightened 13-year-old child sitting on a bank, the enemy convinced me I would be better off dead than alive. That if I were dead, the trauma, the pain, the suffering in my soul would cease. He was a liar from the beginning of time and remains a liar today. And today, even as I am writing this book, I came across this verse in Isaiah:

> They will thrive like watered grass, like willows on a riverbank.
> —Isaiah 44:4 (NLT)

That day, the enemy tried to take my life. As a woman today, the Lord came to give me life. Not only for me, but He promises to pour out His Spirit upon my descendants and His blessing upon my children.

God is faithful and true to undo the works of the enemy and set the captive free. He can bring back to life that which was dead. I know because I am that girl brought back to life.

14 and 15 years old

> I carried both pain and beauty.

This is a tender part of my story, not only to me but to my daughter as well. I want to preface this by saying that my daughter was my first yes to God, one that will forever be my honor. Her life, a blessing in my life. God knew her before she was born; He chose her and chose me to give her life.

> Before I formed you in the womb I knew you.
> —Jeremiah 1:5a (NKJV)

Every smile, every tear, every sound of joy and pain, were each worth the honor of that first yes.

After surviving an attempted suicide, it wasn't long until new depths of dysfunction and trauma came running and seemed to camp out. The sexual, emotional, and physical trauma I went through was intense. It seemed my innocence was gone and so was I. I was lost, unseen, confused, angry, betrayed, rejected, unloved, and unlovable. The things that happened to me are too graphic and painful to write.

I was 14 years old, soon to be 15, and my breasts became very sore. I was sure it was breast cancer. Several years prior to this, my nana had confided in me about the pain in her breast—a knot. She was eventually diagnosed with breast cancer and had surgery to remove her breast. I was certain that was what was going on with me.

I sat in a local health department; we were poor and that was free or low-cost health care. The doctor called my mom and I into her office, and I prepared for the big C word. The doctor looked at me and said that my tests were back, and . . . I was pregnant. I said to her, "Don't you have to want it (sex) to get pregnant?"

I thought sexual intercourse had to be consensual to get pregnant. I didn't know you could become pregnant if they assaulted you and took your innocence. She knew at that point what had happened, and I don't recall her asking questions about it, but I assume she did. I remember sitting across from her in her white coat, unable to look her in the eye. Surely, I thought, I did something to deserve what was done to me.

Fear gripped me, taking my breath, my body and mind paralyzed. Medically, it was shocking that I was able to conceive, especially considering the emotional and physical trauma that had been done to my body from abuse and eating disorders. The doctor told me to come back the next day and they would schedule my abortion. I was already around three months pregnant and needed it done quickly. I asked the doctor what an abortion was. When she briefly explained it to me, I told her that I didn't know if I could do that. She informed me that my only other option was adoption—parenting was not on the table.

I left that office scared and overwhelmed. I didn't go back to see the doctor. I just waited, time passed, and the new life grew inside of me. What I didn't know at the time was the trauma from that incident was significant enough that I would never be able to conceive again. Had I said yes to that doctor, I would have wiped out (at least) two generations. The doctor couldn't have known, but God did.

In the next days, weeks, and months, I don't remember talking about what had happened or was happening. Religious people would stare at me and make terrible, hateful comments. They judged me harshly, but their judgments were misplaced. God, however, did not judge me. He wept with me in the silent moments, though I wouldn't realize this for many years. I believe He caught the tears that fell. I believe His heart ached for the sin that was done to me and that He had already made a way for my heart to heal—His name was and is Jesus.

I tried to do normal things, like going to high school and hanging out with friends, but it was hard. Very hard. One day on the way home on the school bus, I had the strangest thought: "I will give you grace to love your child." I wondered who was speaking. It sounded like me, but I had no idea what it meant. I didn't understand why I needed grace or even what it was. I had no idea at the time that God speaks to your spirit through your thoughts, and His thoughts, His voice, sound like yours. But His thoughts and words bring life. "I will give you grace to love your child." I later learned what grace was and felt immense love for the life growing inside me.

My aunt told me that if I read to my child, he or she would be smart, so I spent time reading my school text books to my unborn baby. I would gently rub, my stomach as I marveled at the growing baby. She moved around and my heart would leap. I would whisper, "I love you." Those words spoken to me from God immediately held power, and a grace was poured over me, though I didn't know what it was.

The day my daughter was born, her beauty captivated my heart. She had slightly olive skin and dark hair like me. She was so small!

And then there was that voice again, "I will give you grace to love your child." I still had no idea it was God speaking. My heart was flooded with love and adoration for her.

She grew and was so beautiful. God did give me grace to love her and eyes to see her always as only my daughter. I never saw her as the product of what had been done to me, but as my child. I loved her.

I will forever remain thankful that I did not listen to the medical community whose first advice was to abort my child. I do not believe we can punish (kill) the child for the sin for the father. If you or someone you know has had an abortion, please know there is grace and forgiveness for you. Jesus wants to give you peace. Find a safe person, ministry, or church to begin the healing journey. Give your unborn baby a name and release all you're carrying. It's not a burden; you have the strength to carry. Invite Jesus into that space of your heart.

The first year of my daughter's life, I strived to do everything perfectly. It felt like I was doing just that, striving. I wanted to be the perfect mother. I gave my daughter all the love I had, though I imagine it was only drops. Then, through a series of very traumatic events that happened to me and those I cared for, I broke. I couldn't cope anymore.

My nana told me I just needed to go to church. I thought she might be right, and church would fix me. I could be a "good Christian," go to church, and read the Bible. But there was so much brokenness inside me. The hymns and religiosity couldn't take away the pain—if anything, it made it worse. I thought I must be broken, beyond help. I tried just sitting and reading the Bible, but it didn't make sense.

Then some people introduced me to ways to forget about the pain and evil happening around me at the time and in the past. Those coping mechanisms weren't good. They even went as far as to show me in the Bible that we were doing was enjoying God's creation. A twisted lie from the enemy. That coping ended up bringing more pain, sorrow, and sin to my life than I ever could have imagined. I didn't think it could get worse, but it did. So much deep-rooted trauma. Nothing seemed to help, and I was spiraling, trying to numb the pain but only making it so much worse. And the worst part of it all was that I had no hope. The Jesus my nana taught me about seemed to love others, but not me.

Chapter Two
Meeting Jesus

> He calmed the storm to a whisper and stilled the waves.
>
> —Psalms 107:29 (NLT)

By the age of 17, my life was a mess. I had hit rock bottom. Coping mechanisms that once brought (what I thought was) peace and the ability to forget all the pain, now only brought more despair. The people I had been hanging around with were older, some *much* older. They were into things that were . . . bad. I started doing what they were doing, going where they were going—places I had no business being. It was a season that ended in devastation. I was alone, broken, and in pain with no hope. It felt like darkness had won . . . again.

One day, I was lying in bed, crying, my heart filled with pain, confusion, and fear. Everything had changed. I was lost in a sea of darkness.

Then . . . Jesus came to me. It was as though He were right in front of me, though I didn't see Him with my eyes, only my heart. He whispered, "Are you tired of running yet?"

It felt like my breath was being gently pulled out of my lungs and given back to me all at the same time. With tears flowing down my cheeks, I said, "Yes, if You can forgive me and give me a new life, I will serve You all my days."

Immediately through Holy Spirit, Jesus came into my heart and made His home with me. Evidence of God came into my life, a sustained joy, a hunger for the word of God, a peace I had never ever felt. God was with me! Immanuel was real and had made His home with me. I was a new person! I had never felt such joy and peace. My circumstances and situation had not changed, but *I had*—I felt it. My soul still needed a lot of work, but my spirit had been awakened.

I want to take a minute and say to you, if you're praying for someone who needs hope, pray for them to come to know Jesus—and don't stop praying! Know that Jesus sits at the right hand of the Father, interceding. Trust Him to intercede for the one you love. Please look into Romans 8:34. I want to encourage you to speak out loud, "I surrender (their name) to You, Jesus. I can't carry them, but You can. I surrender them."

There is power in our words! Speaking their name out loud helps our souls to surrender them. Find someone stronger than you in faith and have them pray too. No matter how hopeless and helpless it may look, don't stop praying, and don't just pray that they go to church. Pray that encounter the living God, because that encounter changes everything. My nana cried out to the One who could save me, and He did.

When Jesus spoke to me, I knew His voice immediately and surrendered my life to Him. I felt His love and His invitation, though I knew I didn't deserve the love and forgiveness He was giving me. It was His mercy and grace that saved me.

> When Jesus heard this, he told them, "Healthy people don't need a doctor—sick people do. I have come to call not those who think they are righteous, but those who know they are sinners."
> —Mark 2:17 (NLT)

I knew I was a sinner. I was a mess, and only God could fix my life. God longs to make His Son known, to bring eternal and abundant life, not just in heaven but here on earth. My life is nothing shy of a miracle. God took a broken girl that was filled with pain and darkness and filled me with light—His Light, His Spirit. He set me on a new path. Jesus came to give us life abundantly. First, we must choose to accept Him as Savior and then welcome Him into places that have pain. If we invite Him, He will come. He always does.

I set apart time each morning to lean into God. He began teaching me His character. He wasn't a condemning God. He was kind and gentle. I could trust Him with my heart. That time with Him taught me how to talk to Him in deeper intimacy, not just asking for something, but talking to Him as a friend. He became my best friend.

Once, when I was still a new Christian, a lady was appalled at how I talked about Jesus. She insisted that He is holy, and I must show reverence—and that's true. I told her, "I *am* showing reverence. He is my best friend, and I can talk to Him just like I'm talking to you." Religious people didn't like me much, but I was so in love with Jesus in my zeal, I just didn't care. I just knew I loved Jesus and He loved me.

I did a lot of Bible Studies. I was in a Baptist one, a Pentecostal one, and a Catholic one. My theology got a little mixed up, but I learned to fall in love with Jesus, the Savior of my heart. The love of Jesus was so compelling that He would leave His father, Heaven and all its glory just to make a way for me to be with Him and give me a life worth living. I couldn't fathom this mercy and grace, even though I received it.

I discovered that God was three Persons: God the Father, God the Son (Jesus), and God the Holy Spirit. I began learning about how God the Father wasn't like earthy fathers, or even the men I had been exposed to. I never knew the love of a Father. I learned that God the Father was good, His love was pure, He wouldn't hurt or abandon me, that He promised, and I could trust Him. He would be my Father and I His daughter. I trusted and took Him at His word.

Chapter Three
Spiritual Mothers and Sisters

Learning to walk with others is a journey.

We need help in our walk with God. We aren't meant to walk alone. God sent my first spiritual mother to me, and she was such a lovely lady. Her joy radiated in her smile. She had deep roots with Jesus and was wise, beautiful, and intelligent. She taught me how to search the Word and talk to Jesus, how to honor God in the little things like drinking enough water for my body, eating well, the importance of exercise, and especially spending time in the Word and worship. She refused to call me by my nickname but insisted on calling me Rebecca. She would say that was the name God gave me. It would be more than 26 years later before I would know the significance of Rebecca. Times with her were a treasure. My life was marked by her love and generosity to me.

Sometime later, I moved and was then discipled by a group of wonderful ladies who hosted a weekly Bible Study. They showed me the love of family, of mothers and sisters. They demonstrated what community looked like. One woman especially loved me deeply, and her heart was always so tender to me; she was incredibly gracious and seemed thankful all the time. Her eyes glistened as she talked about Jesus. I felt she was truly in love with Him, and I wanted to be like that too.

These women showed me how to live as a Christian. I watched them lift their hands to Jesus in worship, dive deep in Bible study, and love each other. I saw them enjoy meals around the table and love the lowly. I knew they were real. They were serious about walking in the freedom. I had told them my story, and they didn't want me going back to bondage and sin. The women taught me serious things like repenting for my sins, asking for forgiveness and releasing forgiveness to others, soul ties, covenants, breaking generational curses, and much more. I knew what the enemy was like, and I wanted nothing to do with him. So, I was all in, hungry to know this freedom they talked about.

I knew the torture in my emotions, the absence of any kind of peace. The thought that death would be better than life. Yet, in their lives, I saw fullness of joy and peace, even in hard times. I was all in to breaking curses, repenting for my sin, and the big one—releasing forgiveness to ALL those who had hurt me. I experienced a lot of freedom, and I received a lot of breakthroughs and revelations through their discipleship.

I realize now that community is pivotal in our walk with the Lord, for accountability and for healing. We are all created for community; we aren't meant to walk alone.

Chapter Four
Divorce and Church Hurt

Let him who is without sin, cast the first stone.

I CONTINUED ATTENDING CHURCH and was serving in many areas. I loved Bible Study and the community of women's group. Life felt good. Then, slowly, my world changed, and it was painful.

I entered a marriage quickly, barely 19 years old. He was older than me. I was searching to be loved and accepted, but wasn't accustomed yet to following Holy Spirit, and I made a terrible mistake by entering this marriage. A mistake that brought such brokenness and destruction to the soul that only God could heal. I bought the lies from the enemy when he said, "This is the only way you'll move forward. He accepted Christ, so he must be okay. God will bless it." These lies took root in my heart. And I followed them.

Entering marriage doesn't fix wounds. It will only compound them. I had no idea so much of what I was fighting, so much of my behavior, was a result of the wounding I had experienced as a child. Marriage was hard. Choices I made and terrible choices he made, the sin done to me and sin I engaged in all played a part. I knew Jesus, had accepted Him as my Savior, yet I had many patterns that needed to be healed.

The obvious path to follow was to dissolve the marriage in divorce. There are many things I wish I had done differently, but had I known then what I know now, I would have never entered into that covenant. I carried so much shame feeling like I had failed. I took on the full responsibility of failing—that was the plan from the enemy, and I bought into it fully.

The Lord would later uncover and reveal, and what was revealed nearly stopped by heart from beating. Yes, He was faithful to remind me that the pain would not take my life, that He would heal and restore, not only me but those I deeply love. The shame I carried? I threw it down like a heavy coat, leaving it at His feet. Divorce no longer defined or disqualified me, but the Lord's delight defined me.

People who called themselves my family, brothers and sisters in the church, judged me harshly, and it hurt me deeply. I had not experienced that kind of hurt from anyone who professed to be a Christian, and I wasn't sure how to process it. It was my first experience with church hurt. People had hurt me, not God, but it was so difficult to separate the two.

After the divorce, there were some who took me by the hand and loved on me. Much of what was said about me wasn't completely true, but it hurt me deeply, and I was so young. The accusations and hurtful words felt like they were bruising my heart. But God pulled me closer and washed the shame and sin off me. Tears would fall in repentance from the way I had hurt God's heart and others'. I spent time repenting for my actions, and the Lord led me in forgiveness for myself and others. He came and healed those places too. He reminded me their gaze wasn't His gaze, their words weren't His words. His grace was real and His love endless.

If you have experienced hurt in or from the church, I want to personally say to you, I am so sorry that happened to you. Church hurt is hard stuff and burns deeply, especially because when one calls themself a Christian, we automatically hold them to a higher standard, expecting them to know better. Many of them are wounded, too, and hurting people hurt people. There is also church hurt from pastors, even abuse. None of which is okay.

In ministering to others, I can tell you wounds received in the church are as significant as wounds received by parents. I want to encourage you to fully forgive, specifically for each offense and wounding you felt. Process that pain with Jesus. We cannot progress in our spiritual walk with God with unresolved conflict and un-forgiveness; it stunts our spiritual growth and delays God's plan for our lives.

> ... So, we must let go of every wound that has pierced us and the sin we so easily fall into. Then we will be able to run life's marathon race with passion and determination, for the path has been already marked out before us. . .
>
> —Hebrews 12:1-2 (TPT)

Life is hard, and we need each other. You may not need to be in fellowship with those who hurt you, but you need to be in fellowship with safe people.

I worked through forgiving those who hurt me, forgiving myself, and restoring my relationship with God. I became intentional about spending time with Him and seeking His heart, releasing the hurt and the lies that God was disappointed in me and was far away. I entered back into fellowship with Him. God led me to a church where it seemed religiosity wasn't present; it was different and enabled me to connect with Him. God began restoring deeper parts of my heart to His. The contemporary worship helped my heart to engage with Holy Spirit.

I had met Jesus, surrendered, and started growing up in the Lord, taking responsibility for my actions and how they impacted others. Soon it would be time to look deep inside my heart at how the actions of others had hurt me. The Lord showed me there was life after divorce, and that divorce didn't define me. Many years later, He showed that His hand was what removed me and saved one from being destroyed, though they were deeply wounded. If you have been through divorce, know that God will give you restoration and healing. You are not marked as bad goods, but chosen for the Lord to heal and restore.

Chapter Five
Cultivating a God Time

Time with God is never time wasted.

BEFORE I WAS ABLE to move into healing my heart, a "God time" had to be established. You need to connect to the only One who can truly heal and restore your heart and soul. This is a glimpse of a God time or better said, a way to build a foundation to start or enhance your God time. This is just the surface of starting this process.

I knew how to have a devotional time—I learned that early in my walk with the Lord. But to really deal with what was happening in my heart, I needed *time* with God, I needed to truly know Him in a deeper capacity, intimately.

> Teach me more about you, how you work and how you move, so that I can walk onward in your truth until everything within me brings honor to your name.
>
> —Psalms 86:11 (TPT)

I have laid some of the ground for what I had to work through, and it was a lot. A God time, a time set with apart just to be with God is a necessity. A time to know Him and His kindness to you. This process will help you to be honest and vulnerable with the painful parts down the road as you learn to fully trust Him.

I will share different facets of what my God time entails. This is not a religious checklist, but just a few of my personal practices and disciplines. These have helped me tremendously in connecting to the heart of God.

I believe we are made up of Spirit (made in the image of God), soul (mind, will & emotions), our body (what you see), and our heart (the seat of being). We were created to be in relationship with God, to commune with Him. Each of us was created with needs that can only be filled by God's love. When we choose to spend time with God, our hearts become positioned to receive His love and that changes everything. If we can receive God's love first, then we can receive love from others. We are meant to experience His love.

> We have come to know [by personal observation and experience], and have believed [with deep, consistent faith] the love which God has for us. God is love, and the one who abides in love abides in God, and God abides continually in him.
> —1 John 4:16 AMP

I want to encourage you to start this for yourself, but keep in mind that it doesn't need to be complicated. Your God time should be a time that you move your heart towards God's heart, where you *enjoy* spending these moments with Him. A time of communing, getting to know Him, feeling His delight over you. For us to have meaningful relationships with anyone, we have to invest time. The more time you invest in your God time, the deeper intimacy with Him will be and the more fruitful your life will become. Experiencing His heart for you changes everything.

Setting a Time

Setting and committing to a time to meet with God is the first step. My phone is set on *do not disturb*, and I have a piece of paper to write down those "don't forget to" thoughts. This is an important time to me as my God time has been my lifeline. I want to give Him my attention, just as I would give attention to my doctor during an appointment. God time is my appointment with Him.

This evolved from a quick 5–10-minute devotional into a space where I'd invest my heart, soul, and time. A time set apart for me to truly know who God is and what He is saying. A space where intimacy with Him was and is the goal. Remember, this intimacy changes absolutely everything. This is a sacred place where His love ministers to my full being—my body, soul, spirit, and heart.

The psalmist penned, "Every morning I move my soul toward Him" so that I can fully connect to God (Psalms 55:17 TPT).

Doing this in the mornings enables me to hear Him throughout the day and sets the tone for the day. I can tell the difference in my day if I don't first meet with God.

A God time truly will make a difference in your life. Just like we will begin to get stronger with consistent exercise, same with our God time. We get spiritually stronger. The more time you commit, the deeper your relationship.

> Every evening, I will explain my need to him. **Every morning, I will move my soul toward him.** Every waking hour I will worship only him, and he will hear and respond to my cry.
> —Psalms 55:17 (TPT)

Start small: decide to wake up 15 minutes early and start the process of building your personal God time. As you begin to experience His love, hear His voice, and feel His kindness, this moves from just something you do to a time you anticipate and participate in.

Acknowledging God

I start my God time by acknowledging Him, His presence, His love for me, His character, and His ways. This started to flow outside of just my God time and into my day, moving my heart and my thoughts to Him throughout each day.

One of the ways we move our hearts to Him is by acknowledging not just what He can do, as we read in Bible stories, but who He is. He is God—He is holy, loving, kind, and generous. He is also the God who sees me and cares deeply for me. The Bible says He sings songs of delight over me and calms my fears with His love. He is the One who, before the foundation of the world, chose me and chose you. He is good and can be trusted.

God is faithful and His love endures forever. He is my safe place, always present, always listening to my heart. I remind my soul of who He is and what He's done in my life, and I remind my heart that I can trust Him because He is a safe place. God will provide for my every need. He is my shalom peace, and He will mend and stitch back together every broken place, because that is His nature. When I position my heart to acknowledge Him, to remember and recall, I can feel God's embrace over my heart, and my faith grows.

I began knowing Who God is by the different names of God. Spend some time researching the names of God. Write down the ones that stand out to you, let them penetrate your heart and touch your vision on how you see Him.

In the very beginning of my God time, acknowledging Him would consist of recalling the miracles He had done, like parting the Red Sea, rescuing His people, winning battles with shouts of praise, turning water into wine, and raising the dead. All of that is important, and we need to know those things because He is the God of miracles, but He is also our kind Creator who yearns for a relationship with us. At first, I only knew what He had done, all the miracles we see in the Bible, so I would acknowledge Him though that lens. Then I begin seeing His love and adoration for me. He began shifting my perspective to who He was to me personally. This helped my heart to engage with Him on a personal level.

One of my favorite verses is, "... She said, 'You are the God who sees me.'" (Genesis 16:13 NLT). He is the God who sees us, who cares. Incorporate into your God time who He is to you and how He cares for you personally. This will help your heart engage on a personal level. Not just by recalling what He has done, but His character and His love, especially for you personally.

> For the Lord your God is living among you. He is a mighty savior. He will take delight in you with gladness. With his love, he will calm all your fears. He will rejoice over you with joyful songs.
> —Zephaniah 3:17 (NLT)

Gratitude

When we pause and shift our hearts to just be grateful, it shifts our perspective and the atmosphere. There are studies that have shown that gratitude can improve our sleep, our moods, and even our immune system. It decreases anxiety, depression, and so much more. But how much more can gratitude do when it's focused on the God of who spun the worlds and hung the stars? The Creator of all.

Shifting our hearts to Him in gratitude changes us—especially gratitude for what He has already done. He is always good and always faithful. Even in the hardest times of my life, when I have paused and just began expressing gratitude for who He is and how He loves me, being grateful for His promises that I can cling to, my heart and perspective shifted. It causes something to happen inside of you. He told me once, "You can trust Me, my DNA is faithfulness." and we certainly can. When I express gratitude that He is faithful, that His eyes are upon me, His gaze fixed on my heart and life, my heart shifts to be able to see the beauty. Gratitude and praise open the door for us to experience heaven; it welcomes His presence. The situation may not change, but we will.

Deep Breaths

A few years ago, I added deep breathing to my God time. This helps to quiet my thoughts and fix my attention on God. To breathe in, as if to breathe in His goodness over me, then to breathe out, releasing all that distracts and overwhelms me. To settle my heart on Him, to give Him my undivided attention, setting my gaze on Jesus.

I began by practicing this for just a few minutes, yielding my heart thoughts to God. Breathing deep and releasing each breath partnered with thoughts of gratitude. I set a timer for two minutes to practice this. When that time was up, my heart and body could feel the peace of God. My thoughts would begin settling and my heart prepared to engage and listen.

As you become comfortable with this process, add a few extra minutes. Train your mind to settle by focusing on who you have come to hear from and be with.

Worship with Song

Worship music is another tool I use. Music helps our heart engage with God; it's the melody that welcomes the Word. I have a playlist of anointed worship leaders, songs that help me to worship God, to move and engage my heart with His. I sing to His heart, and I can feel His love pouring over mine.

I may not listen to music in all of my God time, but it's a tool I use regularly.

A wise man once told me, "Worship prepares our hearts to receive the Word of God." That is so true! Music truly does help our souls and spirits to engage with God. I want to encourage you to let God minister His love to your heart through song and then pour out your adoration to Him. Worship music can help your heart to settle and move your heart to engage with His.

Reading the Bible

This is truly the key, the anchor. Most of the time, I use the verse in my devotional to spur my reading time. Time spent in the Word of God, the scriptures, will strengthen our hearts and give us hope, understanding, and wisdom. The Bible reveals God's character, love, faithfulness, and His plan for our lives. It reveals who He is and who we are, giving us instruction for daily life. The Word teaches us how we should live and treat others, and how they should treat us. It teaches us how to love and reveals what love really looks like. The Bible reveals His history with humanity and teaches us how to trust God. It is the truth. It's where we go when life is difficult and where we go when life is good.

I believe in quality over quantity. There are seasons where I sit and read chapter after chapter and some seasons where I meditate days on just one verse. Holy Spirit is the One that will guide you in that.

> For the word of God is living and active and full of power [making it operative, energizing, and effective]. It is sharper than any two-edged sword, penetrating as far as the division of the soul and spirit [the completeness of a person], and of both joints and marrow [the deepest parts of our nature], exposing and judging the very thoughts and intentions of the heart.
> —Hebrews 4:12 (AMP)

The word of God isn't dead, but alive and active, full of power! God speaks to us through His holy written word. It has stood the test of time and, when applied to our lives, will change us.

> So shall My word be that goes forth from My mouth;
> It shall not return to Me void, But it shall accomplish
> what I please, And it shall prosper in the thing for
> which I sent it.
>
> —Isaiah 55:11 (NKJV)

For years, I have written scriptures on index cards as prayers and declarations. I search the scriptures for promises for my situation, speaking out the word of God over what is happening in my life. When a verse stands out to me, I write it down so I can remind my heart. I keep these scriptures posted around me as reminders of what God has promised and spoken. They remind me of His love for me, His love for those that I love, and ultimately of His promises for situations I am faced with or enduring.

If this is a new process for you, start in the books of Psalms and John. Proverbs is another great book as there are 31 chapters, one for each day. Start slow, letting the words on the page get into your soul. When something sticks out to you, write it down, even adding notes in the margins of your Bible. This will enrich your history with God as you go back and read it. Write down the verses on index cards or sticky notes. This helps me remember throughout the day what God spoke to my heart. When you write them down, add the date (sometimes I add the time as God also speaks in numbers).

Find a translation that you can understand and that you're comfortable with. I encourage you to get a Study Bible, one with good notes that can help you as you begin studying the Word of God. At the time of my writing this book, my favorite is *Spirit Filled Life Bible*; it has entries for words containing the original Hebrew and Greek meanings. For apps, I like the *You Version* app and the *Olive Tree* app. The *Olive Tree* app has the Strong's Concordance that you can purchase with ESV, which I find very helpful. I use a variety of translations, but my go to is the *New Living Translation*.

Chapter Six
Journaling the Voice of God

God desires to speak to you personally.

THIS IS ONE OF my favorites! Journaling God's voice has been huge for me. Every time I sit with God, I journal or write down His voice and words to me.

> But He answered and said, "It is written, 'Man shall not live by bread alone, but by every word that proceeds from the mouth of God.'"
> —Matthew 4:4 (NKJV)

It's an ongoing word spoken from God. We need to read the Bible, the written word of God, to help us discern if what we are journaling is, in fact, God's voice. But we need to hear His voice fresh for each day. Journaling God's voice has been a lifeline for me, like reading the Bible. I sit and record what He is speaking specifically to me, my heart, for that day. This journaling can be on paper, in the notes in your phone, or in a document on your computer. For years, I used a paper journal, though I now use my computer.

I write down the date and something about that day or what's going on in my life. I read a verse and then ask Him to speak, or sometimes I just go right in and ask Him, "God, what do You want to speak to me?" I skip a line, draw a heart (a symbol to me that He was speaking and makes it easy when I go back to see His words), then write down everything I hear in my heart. By faith I start writing. He has always met me there and always spoken to me; it may be only a sentence or two, or sometimes a paragraph or few pages. The more I practiced, the easier it became to hear His voice and what He was saying for my heart for that specific day.

When I first started journaling God's voice, it felt silly. I remember thinking, *is this really God?* Then I noticed His words were softer than mine. They had more kindness towards me than I had for myself. His Words gave me value, hope, encouragement, and sometimes rebuke.

I now have years and years written down of what He has spoken to me. This also helps me with gratitude because I can look back and read His love letters of faithfulness to me. "Is it really God speaking" is answered by determining if it lines up with scripture. God will not speak to you anything that does not line up with His written word. The Bible is our anchor.

A wise man once said to me, "God wants to speak more than we want to listen." Oh how true that is! That same man also told me, "Reading the Bible without asking God what He wants to say is like going to a restaurant and studying the menu, yet never ordering the food." Those words grabbed my heart. That wise man has taught me a lot and holds the tender spot of a father to me. He helped me connect to my heavenly father and taught me how to hear God's voice and write it down. We see this process all throughout the scriptures. God spoke, then man wrote down what God had said.

Another practice I do about once a month is to go back and read what God spoke to me during that month. This always encourages my heart. I do the same at the beginning of the year, looking back though the previous year and reading the words of God to my heart. Where He encouraged me, at times discipled me, each word touching my heart with His adoration for me. Looking back over months and years has been much easier with my computer.

Take time and put into practice this process. Let God speak to your heart. Ask Him how He sees you, then, by faith, start writing.

A Devotional

A good devotional is like having a personal mentor. I have a few devotionals that I switch back and forth between. It's important to find one that is Biblically sound and that you relate to. Devotionals help me tune my heart to hear God for the day. I receive wisdom from someone (the author of the devotional) of what God has spoken to them. It helps you learn from what they have gleaned in their life.

I look up the verse that's referenced, sometimes in multiple translations. I also journal what God wants to say to me through what I've read. Having a solid devotional has been a great teaching tool in my God time. Often, God has used the devotional to address very specific issues I was facing. It truly is like having a personal mentor, one to help explain what you're reading and what the scriptures mean.

Praying in the Spirit

The Bible says in Ephesians 6:18 to pray always in the Spirit (or speaking in tongues). We read in the book of Ephesians how we are to do this constantly, staying alert and persistent. We read in Jude how this builds us up. It enables us to pray the heart of God, to be filled with His strength. I'll share about Baptism of Holy Spirit later in this book. The evidence of "speaking in tongues" is often linked to The Baptism of Holy Spirit.

> Pray in the Spirit at all times and on every occasion. Stay alert and be persistent in your prayers for all believers everywhere.
>
> —Ephesians 6:18 (NLT)

> But you, beloved, building yourselves up on your most holy faith, praying in the Holy Spirit.
> —Jude 20 (NKJV)

There have been times while I sat praying in the Spirit that I could literally feel the strength of God empowering my heart. When someone asks me to pray for them, I will pray in the Spirit over them, as I believe this is me aligning my prayers to the heart of God and what His plan and will is. I remember the time my friend prayed over my heart in tongues, how I felt the power of God stirring my heart as if it were water being stirred. It's a powerful tool that is a gift from heaven.

When you practice this often, it can be as natural as praying in your first language (for me, that's English).

Prayer

Our God time is a time we are communing with Him. Engaging in prayer is having a conversation with God. Prayer is sharing our hearts and sometimes sitting together with Him in silence, listening to His heart. Prayer is two-way—us speaking to God, and God speaking to us. It's a conversation.

Prayer isn't just in my God time but throughout my day. It's ongoing, as natural as breathing to me. Prayer isn't just speaking but listening to what the Father is speaking. What is He saying?

Where is He leading your heart? Learning to be still and listen is powerful.

> Surely I have calmed and quieted my soul, Like a weaned child with his mother; Like a weaned child is my soul within me.
> —Psalms 131:2 (NKJV)

> Be still and know (recognize, understand) that I am God.
> —Psalms 46:10a (AMP)

The most important "work" we will ever do is pray. Prayer is us connecting with God, and that is the greatest of all works. The one thing the disciples asked Jesus to teach them was not how to perform miracles or cast out devils. They asked Him to teach them how to pray.

In this manner, therefore, pray:

> Our Father in heaven,
> Hallowed be Your name.
> Your kingdom come.
> Your will be done
> On earth as it is in heaven.
> Give us this day our daily bread.
> And forgive us our debts,

> As we forgive our debtors.
> And do not lead us into temptation,
> But deliver us from the evil one.
> For Yours is the kingdom and the power and the glory forever. Amen.
> —Matthew 6:9-13 (NKJV)

The disciples watched Jesus slip off to a quiet place, an isolated place, to engage with His Father, who, through the blood of Jesus, is now our Father.

> Before daybreak the next morning, Jesus got up and went out to an isolated place to pray.
> —Mark 1:35 (NLT)

During prayer, our hearts join with God's and seek His plan, His will. This sacred and holy process is also one that the youngest of children can engage in. Prayer helps our hearts to delight in Him as He delights in us.

Intercessory Prayer and Praying for Others

This isn't so much a part of my morning God time, but my daily life as a whole, and is very important.

There are parts of my prayer time where I pray for people, interceding for them and lifting each person that God brings to my heart and mind. I take time to ask Him what He wants me to pray over them. If we ask Him, He will speak. I pray scriptures over them and their situations, and I depend on Holy Spirit to lead me in this time because I need His guidance on how to pray.

Sometimes the prayer is very specific. At other times it is general but equally important. If I take the time to ask God what and how to pray, this helps alleviate prayers from my soul and emotions. Sometimes a prayer from the depth of your emotions is exactly what's needed, but there are times where if we pray from our emotions, or our souls, that we can be praying outside the will of God; we don't always know the will of God, but Holy Spirit does.

I prayed as God prompted me for years. Especially for my family and friends, then the specifics of what and whom I was praying for began to shift. One of my first encounters with this shift was with the wise man I spoke about earlier. God impressed on my heart to pray over him, his family, and ministry daily. Holy Spirit would guide me very specifically with what to pray. I wouldn't be able to confirm if I was hearing God correctly in my prayers, as he didn't know me or even that I was praying. It was an assignment between God and me. One day in a large supermarket, I saw him and his darling wife, and I shared that I pray for him daily. Eventually I would share with him about the specific prayers, and many times we could confirm "that prayer is spot on." It has been an honor to pray and intercede over them.

Another encounter of intercessory prayers occurred many years ago. It was time for my lunch break, so I left work and headed home since I lived just a mile from my office. I was reading the

Bible and praying when all of the sudden, it was as though I was literally standing in some kind of hut. The floor was dirt, and in front of me was a woman with a very dark complexation holding her crying baby, tears streaming down her face. I could feel the starvation of her child in my own body, the hunger pains the child felt and the desperation from the mother. I knew exactly how to pray. Through sobs, I began interceding for the woman and her the child, praying in the spirit. I knew that God had invited me into a sacred space, and I stayed in that place until I could feel the burden lift. That prayer time marked me. It was days before I could even speak about it, and even then my voice would crack through the tears.

There have been many times when I became so overwhelmed in my emotions as Holy Spirit led me into prayer and intercession for others. It's difficult to explain. The first time this happened, it was so painful that the only thing I can compare it to would be receiving the news someone you deeply love has passed away. Deep anguish.

One time that this emotional episode came over me, I laid on my floor for two hours, sobbing and praying in the spirit. This one was hard, as I knew who I was praying for, though I wasn't sure what exactly I was praying about—God knew, I was certain of that. A few days later, I received a message about a terrible event that had occurred the evening I had been praying. This type of intense prayer has happened to me many times. I've learned when it "feels" different. Most of the time, I don't have a good reason for the emotions I'm feeling. I just know that I feel it deeply, so I've learned when this strong feeling comes over me, to rush to the

Father as He has entrusted me to pray for what is important to His heart. God has also taught me the value of feeling or the value of my emotions. He made them and will use them.

Prayer is powerful. I saw that when I was 13 years old when I woke up from the coma with my nana's pastor praying over me. I have seen the power of God move mountains; it's sacred and holy. It is not meant to be intimating but welcoming us into a space with God. When Holy Spirit prompts us to pray, we need to be obedient as only He knows the depth of the situation.

Intercessory prayer isn't a prayer for the dining room table before a meal, but prayer for the secret place. It is real and powerful. We welcome the Spirit of God to come and lead us in what He wants us to intercede in, and it's a powerful process.

In Conclusion

Don't let your God time become a religious check-off, but a time of intimacy where you realize you are known to Him and He becomes known to you. God isn't far off or out of reach. He is closer than your breath and desires a personal, intimate time with you. This is where you know His thoughts for you and receive His strength for anything you may be facing. It is a space where you receive His peace and joy over your day and life.

> For the Lord your God is living among you. He is a mighty savior. He will take delight in you with gladness. With his love, he will calm all your fears. He will rejoice over you with joyful songs.
> —Zephaniah 3:17 (NLT)

God truly is in our midst, living among us. He is mighty savior, taking delight in you. He is rejoicing over you with gladness, quieting your fears with His love, and singing over you. His heart is opposite from what many religions teach, which would have us work for His attention and affection. Relationship will pull our heart to His, so we are aware of His attention and receive His affection for our hearts.

A God time is the most important thing you can do in the Kingdom of God—more than going to church, serving, or doing missionary work. A time that you close off all distractions to meet with the God, who spun the planets into orbit and called the stars by name, and yet sees you and desires to reveal His heart to you.

One morning, I woke up and saw Jesus sitting at the foot of my bed, and He said, "I've been waiting for you." My heart was elated, and the love radiating and filling the room was indescribable. He enjoys my time with Him just as much, if not more than, I do. God is love, and He is patient and understanding, inviting us to sit with Him, to hear His voice.

This week, take time to pause and sit in His presence. Commit to waking up 15-20 minutes early to begin cultivating your own personal God time. Come, sit with a heart that simply says yes to meeting with Him. Bring your Bible, journal, and pen (or computer with notifications silenced), and a devotional.

Commit your time to God. Start by praying, "Lord, I give You space and permission to do what You want. This is Your time. I come to sit at Your feet to hear Your heart. I shift all my focus to You."

Start with a few deep breaths to settle your heart. Breathe in and then out, and say, "Thank You. Thank You Lord for all you do for me, that You're with me."

Get your Bible and devotional out, and ask Holy Spirit to give you understanding. Read the devotional for that day, the open your Bible and look up the verse that was referenced. As you read, look for ways you can implement the wisdom in the devotional in your own life.

Ask God what He wants to say to you and then write everything down. Listen to a worship song that draws your heart to His. Rest in His presence, and allow Him to fill your heart with the love you so desperately need.

Welcome His Spirit into your life. Go to Him. Let Him wash away any heaviness you have been carrying.

> Come to Me, all you who labor and are heavy laden, and I will give you rest. Take My yoke upon you and learn from Me, for I am gentle and lowly in heart, and you will find rest for your souls. For My yoke *is* easy and My burden is light."
>
> —Matthew 11:28-30 (NKJV)

Meeting Holy Spirit

> And I will ask the Father, and He will give you another Helper (Comforter, Advocate, Intercessor—Counselor, Strengthener, Standby), to be with you forever—the Spirit of Truth, whom the world cannot receive [and take to its heart] because it does not see Him or know Him, *but* you know Him because He (the Holy Spirit) remains with you *continually* and will be in you.
>
> —John 14:16-17 (AMP)

We were attending a local non-denominational church, and God brought another spiritual mother into my life. The pastor asked me to meet with her because she wanted to start a prayer group in our church. She first became a friend, then eventually like a spiritual mother to me. She taught and nurtured me in the Lord and shared about Holy Spirit and her experiencing the moves of

God in her life. I was curious and wanted to see the moves of God too. I didn't really know Holy Spirit in that way.

One day, I got news that shook me to my core. I sat in her car crying and said, "I just can't do this again."

With such a calm demeanor she said, "Yes, you can. God is with you."

A situation then occurred in my life that, to me, felt like life or death. I became so desperate for God to move. I *needed* Him. I was reading through scripture about praying in different languages, where Holy Spirit would pray through us with words we couldn't even understand. I desperately needed God's Words. My prayers felt like they were lacking power, as though they were hitting the ceiling and falling back down. I began reading the book of Acts without the lens of tradition, but with a new lens of "Teach me God, I am Your student." Then, I would be introduced to God though baptism, not with water, but the baptism of Holy Spirit and, eventually, fire.

> "I (John) baptize with water those who repent of their sins and turn to God. But someone is coming soon who is greater than I am—so much greater that I'm not worthy even to be His slave and carry His sandals. He will baptize you with the Holy Spirit and with fire."
>
> —Matthew 3:11 (NLT)

I was picking up a friend and her daughter to take them home. My friend asked me how things were going, and I began sobbing, so overwhelmed and scared at what might happen. As I pulled up to drop them off, my friend asked if she could pray for my situation. I welcomed her heart and prayers. She then asked if she could pray in tongues, and while I didn't know exactly what that was, I knew and trusted her, so I said yes. As she prayed, I could feel the power of God come into my car. Holy Spirit came and consumed the air, yet breathing was effortless. I felt the power of God so strongly, but not like at church—this was different. It was His presence. As she finished praying, her daughter woke up from her nap. I hugged them goodbye and thanked my friend for praying over us.

On the way home, I was worshipping Jesus, speaking out loud "hallelujah" over and over, because I had read or heard that was the highest form of praise I could give Him. As I did, my body became extremely hot. A syllable came out of my mouth that I didn't know, kind of like when a baby is learning to first speak. I felt the power of God in and through me, and also all around me. He had come and consumed the space again. Sobs flowed out of me, tears flooded my cheeks, and a new language exploded from my lips.

I worshiped Him with all my heart. I turned the air conditioning up as high as it would go, yet the heat I was experiencing did not go away. I had never felt anything like it. I got home and wondered how I would explain this to my husband. So I went out for a run, and when I got back, I said, "I have something to share with you." When I shared with him this story, he told me he didn't know what it all was, but he knew my character and knew me.

In my God time when I worshipped Him, I would speak out my syllable, and that syllable eventually became an entire language. When I prayed in my heavenly language, I could feel a new strength come from heaven, empowering me. Long before I had that language, I had asked God the Father to fill me with Holy Spirit, like I had read in the book of Acts.

As Jesus baptized me with Holy Spirit, my life radically changed again. Hope felt strong, not lost. I had no idea how to explain what had happened to me, so I asked God, "How do I explain this?"

I had been a Christian for years, yet I had never experienced anything like this. God replied, "It's like going from black and white to color, isn't it?"

Yes, it certainly was! My world went from black and white to color. I became so hungry for God, what He was doing, what He was saying. The feeling inside of me was like electricity. A new boldness came, a deep hunger for God, a deeper strength. I wanted everyone to be baptized with Holy Spirit. In my zeal, some were turned away, but my heart was for them to receive this new strength and power.

> "And now I will send the Holy Spirit, just as my Father promised. But stay here in the city until the Holy Spirit comes and fills you with power from heaven."
> —Luke 24:49 (NLT)

> And everyone present was filled with the Holy Spirit and began speaking in other languages, as the Holy Spirit gave them this ability.
>
> —Acts 2:4 (NLT)

Life was at a new level as I felt the power of God in my life. Baptism of Holy Spirit did not burn up my pain, but it gave me a new strength to press into what He was soon going to call me deeper into. It was like Holy Spirit joined with my spirit when I gave my life to Jesus, but when He baptized me, it was like it flowed into my soul. As if to go from being with me to in me, and all my senses were touched. I began to see visions and have dreams from God. I could feel His presence as if He was standing right beside me. I experienced Him in my daily walk. If you have not had this experience, I want to encourage you to ask God for baptism of Holy Spirit and ask that He come and baptize you with fire and fill you.

I finally had a new strength to go deeper with Jesus; I had a helper and a counselor.

> And I will ask the Father, and He will give you another Helper (Comforter, Advocate, Intercessor—Counselor, Strengthener, Standby), to be with you forever— the Spirit of Truth, whom the world cannot receive [and take to its heart] because it does not see Him or know Him, *but* you know Him because He (the Holy Spirit) remains with you *continually* and will be in you.
>
> —John 14:16-17 (AMP)

Holy Spirit had filled me, and I felt like a whole new person, a rebirth. I didn't know a lot about healing the heart, or inner healing as some call it. I still stuffed down any resemblance of pain, rebuking it as "It must be the enemy trying to attack me. I must forget the past and press into the future"—though that verse is used out of context so often.

I did what I thought I was supposed to do, and buried my pain. I declared scripture and worshiped God, I listened to only anointed Christian worship, I had a new level of freedom, and I was experiencing God. Yet, I ignored every bit of the pain in my heart and soul. That is what I thought all Christians did, at least the ones I was around. That process kept me in coping, not healing, though I wouldn't know it was coping for quite some time.

Testimony of Journaling God's Voice

> My own sheep will hear my voice and I know each one, and they will follow me.
> —John 10:27 (TPT)

> But He answered and said, "It is written, 'Man shall not live by bread alone, but by every word that proceeds from the mouth of God."
> —Matthew 4:4 (NKJV)

When we spend time with God, we learn to hear and discern His voice. It's like our hearts begin to tune into His voice. We need to write down what He is speaking specifically to our heart for that day.

As I shared in the beginning, I grew up partially with my mom and stepfather and partially with my grandparents, Nana and Pawpaw. My grandfather passed away when I was nine years old, so then it just my Nana.

At the time of my birth, my mother was legally married, though separated. Due to the laws in the state where we lived, I was given the surname of her husband, and his name was added to my birth certificate. Because he didn't legally contest being my biological father, and DNA tests were not requested, his name remained on my birth certificate for almost 39 years.

When I was at my grandmother's home, which was most of my life, he lived a few miles away from me. We would pass the road he lived on when we went to get the mail or groceries, and I remember being on the school bus, his children walking past me as they got off the bus. Constant reminders of the lack of him as a father in my life.

As a little girl, I asked my grandmother, "Why don't I look like them?" They had red hair, freckles, and very Caucasian skin. She would just say, "Well, you just look like me." That was true—my dark brown eyes matched hers, and so did my olive complexion.

I still felt the deep wound of rejection. "Why didn't my father love me? Why was I so unlovable? What did his other children have that I didn't?" Later, I had a deep feeling in my soul that I truly wasn't his child. I began asking my mom about it. She would get so angry and say to me, "Yes, he is your father, now don't ask me again." By adulthood I was sure he wasn't my biological father. I could just feel it.

At times in my life, I would begin to wonder about who my biological father really was. I would think on it and then dismiss it, burying the thoughts and feelings. Then it would come up again, so I'd ask my mom, and she'd get angry with for me asking again. But those deep feelings kept surfacing, and I wondered things like, "Do I look like him?" I wanted to look like somebody. I felt that if I looked like someone, I would feel some belonging in a family, that I would *feel* the emotional need I had for acceptance and affirmation.

Then, on November 14, 2017, my life changed. I journaled to God: "This morning, I just wanted to sleep. I'm so tired, worn out, and exhausted. I knew You'd be waiting for me. Thank You for helping me to fight the urge to lay back down. I love You, Papa."

I then read Bible passage Genesis 24 and wrote the following: "Genesis 24. What a beautiful story of Abraham's servant finding a wife for Isaac."

> "Praise the Lord, the God of my master, Abraham," he said. "The Lord has shown unfailing love and faithfulness to my master, for he has led me straight to my master's relatives."
> —Genesis 24:27 (NLT)

The story in Genesis felt like an open door to something so special and sacred. I wrote, "God, is there something you want to speak to me?"

God spoke to me, "I will bring your father straight to you."

As I penned those words, my heart was pounding. I texted my best friend, "Could this really be God speaking? Is this God?" She replied with such kindness. "Leave it with the Lord. If it's Him, it will come to pass. If not, it will fall to the ground." I was so afraid of disappointment, scared to even ask my mom again.

God spoke again, "... leave your heart, fear of disappointment in My hands and ask her again."

My heart was still pounding so hard, it felt like it would jump out of my chest. God had just told me that He would bring my father straight to me.

During a Thanksgiving meal, I took a deep breath and asked my mom for a name. Same story ... she got angry. "The man on your birth certificate is your father."

By this time, he had died. I responded to her, "No, he's not. God told me He would bring my father straight to me. I forgave you a long time ago for lying to me, but I need my father's name. Think on it, and we'll talk about it later." You could have heard a pin drop as a deep seriousness filled the room. I walked away and took a few deep breaths, trusting God yet still fighting fear tears.

I wondered for days if she would tell me who he is. I had thought that maybe he was a man I saw a lot as a child. I wondered if I was the result of an affair, and that was why he had abandoned me. A week went by, and I was still waiting. My daughter called my mom and told her she was tired of waiting and asked for a name. My daughter then called me at work, but I texted her back that I was in a meeting. Her response was, "I found your father."

The text contained the name of a man and an address. I hung up from my meeting and rushed home. I was staring at a name I had never heard, and the address was only about 45 minutes from my house (which was 10-15 minutes from where I grew up). And that got my heart pounding again.

I called my mom and asked her about this name. She told me a very detailed story about him, including how they met, She said, "He was the kindest man I had ever met." I was beyond shocked. I called the number that my daughter gave me, but no one answered. My husband told me I should think about what I was going to say. I mean, what *do* you say? Well, Holy Spirit told me exactly what to say.

About an hour later, I called back, and a lady answered. I asked for the man, and she confirmed that he was her husband and this was his number, but he was at church. She wanted to know why I was calling. I told her that I had questions I was hoping he could answer. She was very kind to me, and we talked for about 20 minutes.

Towards the end of our conversation, she said, "Can I ask you a question?"

"Sure."

"Are you Hispanic?"

"No."

"Do you look Hispanic?"

I knew what she meant, she was asking if I thought her husband was my father. I replied, "I don't know if I look Hispanic. I have brown eyes and olive skin, but so does my nana." She assured me that she would have him call me. I told her he could call me no matter what time he got home.

I waited by the phone, and later that night, he called me back. My hands trembled as I answered the phone. He wanted to know who I was and why I was calling, so I told him my name and the name of my mom. Immediately, almost verbatim, he began telling me the same stories she had told me earlier. I was blown away.

He then asked me, "Is your mom sick?"
"No."
"Is she dead?"
"No."
"Then why are you calling."
I took a deep breath and replied, "I think you're my father."

Once again, you could have heard a pin drop. It felt like the oxygen was being sucked out of the room. I had never said those words to anyone, and they shook me to my core.

He replied in Spanish-English slang, but it translated to, "What you say baby, what you say?"

"I think you're my father."

"Oh, no, I'm not your father." Sobs nearly burst out of me. He continued, "But tell me where you live, and I'll come straight to you."

He had spoken to me the exact words of what God had promised. We set a time and place for the next day.

On the way to meet him the next morning, I called my mom. I told her that I had spoken to him and that I needed the truth, because he has a wife, a family. I was so afraid she was lying to me, and I felt a responsibility for what I might be doing to their family. And if he wasn't my father, I didn't think I could handle it. I hung up with my mom and prayed, "Holy Spirit, could You give me some kind of sign to show me if this man is my father?"

I told him that I would be wearing a white wool coat. I arrived 45 minutes early, but apparently, they had arrived about 15 minutes before me. I sat in my car looking for anyone that may match what I expected them to look like in my head. After about 40 minutes, I walked up and stood in front of the restaurant. His wife came out and told me they were inside, so I followed her in.

I sat beside him, visibly shaking. Fear and panic fought to come forth. I looked at his wife and saw that she was wearing a cross necklace, so I asked if I could pray for us. They didn't mind. I prayed for the Spirit of Truth, Holy Spirit, to come and bring truth and peace.

> He then looked at his wife and said, "I don't know . . . maybe I *am* her father."

She asked him, "Does she look like someone you know?"
He said yes, his sister.

I then noticed this little nodule thing on his ear; it was exactly like the ones I have! I looked at his wife and asked to see her ears. Puzzled, she asked why as she tucked her hair behind her ears. I pulled my hair back and said, "Look, my ears are like his." I had been teased terribly throughout school, called names and mocked for the nodules on my ears. God was getting ready to use what the enemy had used to hurt me, but He would bring a breath of peace that would be a staple in my thoughts.

I asked them for a DNA test and told them I would pay for it. At that, his wife said, "Yes, I think we need to do that."

It was the weekend, so the next couple of days would be difficult. When Monday morning came, I called my doctor's office, and a lady there connected me with the appropriate people. Soon, we went and completed the DNA test. So many thoughts swirled around me. Was he my father? If not, then who could it be?

After we completed our DNA tests, we went to grab some lunch, and he insisted on buying my meal. I ordered my food, but when they brought it to the table, they brought me a kid's meal. There I sat, after having the DNA test, in front of the man who was potentially my father, eating a kid's meal. God has such a sense of humor sometimes.

He looked at me, and I'm sure my face revealed all the emotions I was feeling: fear, anxiety, uncertainty, possibly hope. Yet, I truly didn't think I *needed* a father—after all, God was my father. I never knew there were wounds from not having a father as a little girl, but after meeting him, his kindness captured my heart.

With my emotions swirling, he said, "We do not worry and we do not fret. We trust in our God." His words seemed to wrap my soul in peace. Then he wrote down verses on a piece of paper. I still have that paper. The unique thing is, that's the same thing I had done for friends and family—writing down verses for them that would help bring peace to their hearts.

The next week was so emotionally taxing as we waited for the results; the uncertainty plagued me. I had no idea of the emotional weight that I would carry. I talked to his wife every few days. She was really kind to me and told me if he wasn't my father, that she would do all she could to help me find out who was. The night before we got the DNA results, I came home from work with a deep heaviness upon me. The best way I can describe it is like the blanket placed on your chest at the dentist's office before having x-rays. The heaviness was intense.

As I laid down, God spoke to me, "Beloved, that is what his wife is going to feel. I need you to pray for her." I had experienced deep intercession with Holy Spirit before and recognized this urgency inside my heart. I feel asleep praying over her.

That next day, I received a call, my heart racing when I saw the number that popped up. I answered, and the man on the other end told me that the DNA tests had confirmed he was my father. God had brought my Father straight to me. I called right away and was able to give him the results. He began praising God for bringing me to him.

Journaling God's voice that morning changed my life and the lives of my family. All initiated through journaling God's voice, matching His voice to scripture, and giving God a mustard seed of faith. A few days later, my dad, his wife, and myself made plans for me to spend time with them. We went to a special restaurant, and walked in at 1:50 for a late lunch, having no idea they closed at 2:00. They were so gracious to us. I sat there in a restaurant where no one was allowed to enter and shared our first meal while knowing I was my father's daughter. It was so very special.

I went back to their home and looked at pictures as he shared about our family. The words, "I have waited 38.5 years for your voice" came out of my heart, and tears rushed down my cheeks. I had no idea the pain that I had buried. I didn't realize that I needed a father. Jesus would then begin healing the parts of my heart where the pain had been hidden for decades.

In my opinion, journaling God's voice is the key to intimacy in our God time.

Remember, that wise man once said to me, "God wants to speak to us more than we want to listen." We want to listen to God when it's convenient, or we don't want to do the work of being still. The morning that God told me He would bring my father to me, all I truly wanted to do was sleep, but I had made it a discipline to spend time with God, and God met with reward. God wants to speak to our hearts. To share His thoughts, plans, and love with us. To touch and heal the places that needs heaven. He wants to touch places that need the healing that only He can bring.

> But He answered and said, "It is written, 'Man shall not live by bread alone, but by every word that proceeds from the mouth of God."
> —Matthew 4:4 (NKJV)

> My own sheep will hear my voice and I know each one, and they will follow me.
>
> —John 10:27 (TPT)

If you have accepted Jesus as your personal Savior, you are then His sheep and hear His voice, though you may not realize it. The more you practice, the easier it becomes to hear what He is saying to you. In everything, God has a voice. You can hear Him in anything or miss Him in everything.

Years ago, those words changed how I perceived things around me. I begin seeking His voice and slowing down my heart to hear His. God truly does want to speak to us more than we want to listen. Slow down and ask Him to speak, to reveal His heart to you. He will always show up. As I began the journey of slowing down, my heart opened to hear Him more. I began to hear Him in nature and things around me, even in something someone would say, like numbers. His voice is always speaking.

Jesus is the One who sees and cares, the God who tends to my soul. He is the kind Guardian who lovingly watches over our souls.

> . . . but now you have returned to the true Shepherd of your lives—the kind Guardian who lovingly watches over your souls.
>
> —1 Peter 2:25 (TPT)

PROMPT:

Start a journal (or if you already have one, then continue in your journal) and add the date, something about the day or your life, and what spoke to you in the devotional or the scripture reading. Then ask, "Lord, what do You want to say to Me?" Write down everything He says.

The way we know if it's God's voice is by asking if it lines up with scripture. Another way for me personally was recognizing His words to me were softer than the words I would speak to myself. God will never speak to you anything that is against the Bible, the written word of God. When God spoke to me that He would bring my father to me, it was the actual verse! I took my best friend's advice and lifted that up to the Lord, saying, "Lord, if it's Your voice, it will happen, and if not, it won't—but I trust you." Spend time reading His written word, the Bible. This will help your spirit connect to His and bring a deeper understanding of who God is. Remember, you can start your God time with a worship song to help your heart connect to His.

If you have not accepted Jesus into your life or surrendered your life to Him, I want to invite you to do that now. God loves you personally, and He desires a relationship with you. It doesn't matter what your past is or what you've done—God loves you and wants a relationship with you. If you want to receive Jesus into your heart and life, I encourage you to pray this prayer:

God, I come to You now in the name of Jesus. I confess that I have sinned. I have not lived my life for You, but I ask now, God, for Your forgiveness of all my sins. I believe that Jesus is the Son of God, and He died on the cross for my sins to be forgiven. I accept Your forgiveness now. I choose to make Jesus Lord of my life, following Him from this day forth. I ask for Your Spirit to come fill me and help me. I pray all of this in the name of Jesus. Amen.

If this was your first time praying this prayer, I want to encourage you to share this with someone. Find a local church; you may need to visit a few, but find a local body of believers to plug in to. I celebrate with Heaven your new life!

Chapter Seven

44

In order to walk through the door of our future, we must first walk through the door in our past.

THE NUMBER 44 REPRESENTS a deep healing journey that Jesus invited and welcomed me into. It was as though He held out His hand to me, welcoming me into a space that He consumed with His love.

I love numbers. I have for a long time. God loves numbers too—he included a book in the Bible called Numbers. Some time ago, I noticed I had been seeing the number 44 often. In the beginning it was kind of subtle. I would see it once, and then a little while later, I'd see it again. Then I began realizing, "I've seen the number 44 a lot today." Then I began seeing it all around me. I would be driving, and the license plate of a nearby car would have it. I would pass a gas station that included gas prices with the number 44 in them, or see commercials with phone numbers ending in 44, or come across page numbers.

One of my favorite times is when I was updating a spreadsheet, and I entered a number (there wasn't anything special about it). As soon as I entered it, the formula populated the number 44 into about 100 cells. I knew that was God getting my attention, though I wasn't sure what it was about. I began moving my heart to the Father when I'd see 44, inviting Him to teach me and speak what He wanted me to learn.

I spent time looking up verse after verse in the Bible that had a 44, searching out what God was speaking to me. I found wonderful verses that encouraged my heart, but nothing that just grabbed me like, "That's it!" There had to be more. I had no idea what 44 meant, but I knew it was significant.

A friend connected me with someone who knew about numbers. She shared how he was familiar with Hebrew and that he could possibly help me. When I spoke with him, he shared that the Hebrew alphabet was made up of words, pictures (which can truly speak a thousand words), and numbers. I was so intrigued! He shared that the 4 in Hebrew was called a *Dalet* and the picture was a door. I could feel the imagery of a door was significant, but I had no answers as to what the significance was.

I asked him what he thought the 44 meant for me personally. A few days later he reached out to me and shared that he had a word from God for me. We met via Zoom, and he began to share again about how the *Dalet*, when written out, looks like a door. He shared with me that God had given him a passage from the Bible. This had my attention, as God knew I love His word; it is our anchor, the Truth. Many times, when someone shares something with me, I want to know where it is in scripture. When reading the scriptures, we need to dig deeper to find the original Hebrew, Greek, and Aramaic meaning to understand what God wants to speak to you. We also need to study that time and culture.

He continued on that the 44 was a double door, that what I was seeing wasn't just 44, but two 4s. Then he read from the Bible.

So, Lot stepped outside to talk to them, shutting the door behind him.
"Stand back!" they shouted. "This fellow came to town as an outsider, and now he's acting like our judge! We'll treat you far worse than those other men!" And they lunged toward Lot to break down the door.

> But the two angels reached out, pulled Lot into the house, and bolted the door. Then they blinded all the men, young and old, who were at the door of the house, so they gave up trying to get inside.
> —Genesis 19:6, 9-11 (NLT)

As he read, I caught the references to doors and leaned in deeper to listen. He continued to read the passage in Genesis 16 about the men in the city desiring to sexually abuse the angels, and how Lot protected them by bringing them inside and closing the door behind them. Tears came to my eyes, and the emotions felt like they would choke me. I knew this was certainly a word from God. He continued speaking, sharing how God had allowed him to feel the fear and insecurity that I felt as a little girl. As he spoke those words to me, it was all I could do not to fall apart.

I had experienced a lot of healing and truly thought I was healed of all past hurts. What I now realize is I had forgiven much. Forgiveness doesn't equal healing, but you can't heal without forgiveness.

I had forgiven these men and those I held responsible for hurting me, but I could feel that God wanted to take me to a deeper place. The tears flowing inside my heart and the shaking inside my body was evidence that more healing was needed.

The first 4 was the door to my past. I knew God meant past as in the abuse and trauma I had endured—I believe that's why God gave him the passage in Genesis 19. The second 4 was my future. When the man said to me, "It was so vivid, I felt like I was there with you in your past, the feeling of insecurity and fear," it was like Jesus had sent someone who could comfort me and validate my pain that was hidden from others, but not hidden from God. The man shared that he had asked his wife if he, as a male, should be the one to share this word with me. I'm so glad he did, as his tenderness to me felt like a father's love.

I took what he had shared with me that day back to my God time. I knew that God was going to bring a deeper healing to my past so I could walk through the door of my future, the door He had and still has for me. I journaled God's voice for my heart, and I began studying the Hebrew alphabet. The meanings behind numbers and pictures were astounding to me. I could study for hours and hours and barely scratch the surface. The 44 is a massive number with deep meanings, and as I continued studying, God revealed more and more to my heart.

> Call to Me and I will answer you, and tell you [and even show you] great and mighty things, [things which have been confined and hidden], which you not know *and* understand *and* cannot distinguish.
> —Jeremiah 33:3 (AMP)

I began seeing lots of numbers, God would grab my attention when they were in double digits. I also frequently saw 55 around time when I first started seeing 44. I shared that with the man who helped me with 44, and he said that he felt the 55 had something to do with healing in my body. He was right! The more I dug deep into healing my heart, my body started healing. It was so little at first, I didn't even recognize it. I sat with the Lord . . . well, He sat with me. I allowed Holy Spirit to move and have His way, and the deeper we went, the more healing that came.

> He sent out his word and healed them, snatching them from the door of death.
> —Psalms 107:20 (NLT)

Numbers have held meant different meanings in different seasons in my life, just like a Bible verse does.

PROMPT:

Start paying more attention to your surroundings to see if God is showing you any numbers repeatedly. Mine started with the double digits 44, then came 55 and 22.

Begin studying the numbers you're seeing in Hebrew. Start a notebook (online or on paper), and as you look up the number(s), make notes of what stands out to you. Ask Holy Spirit what He wants to say to you. I keep a separate journal for numbers.

I do want to give a warning—do not go into numerology, because that's not of God, but is rooted in the occult and witchcraft. If you have sought numerology, I want to encourage you to repent, even if you didn't realize it wasn't of God. My prayer would be something like this:

God, I repent for seeking answers outside of You. In the name of Jesus, I ask You to forgive me for seeking numerology. I choose to turn away from that now. Through the blood of Jesus, I close every door opened to the enemy in Jesus' name.

Chapter Eight
Jehovah Rapha

He sent out his word and healed them, snatching them from the door of death.

I was working on healing my heart, allowing Holy Spirit to help me process and dig deep into painful situations and memories. Healing is a word with so many meanings from so many places. Depending on who you ask, you'll get different definitions. My question is how does God define healing? What is His language? These are the questions to ask ourselves.

What I learned is that healing is a person, Jehovah Rapha, one of the names of God. He is the God who heals—physically, mentally, emotionally, and spiritually. He is the God who heals the whole person, He is the One who knit us together in our mother's womb.

> You made all the delicate, **inner** parts of my body and knit me together in my mother's womb.
> —Psalms 139:13 (NLT)

The word "inner" in this verse in Hebrew is *kilya*, which can be translated as "the seat of the emotion and affection, or mind." I believe this is where God is saying He knit together your body, soul, and heart. The Bible says we are made in the image of God. God is spirit, therefore, we are too.

We are three parts: body, soul, and spirit in the seat of our innermost being, our heart. God made each of these. He created and desired to protect our hearts even in our mother's womb. He cares deeply for our hearts, even though we can experience rejection, pain, and sorrow. I do not believe this was or is God's plan. We've already addressed John 10:10, but this is where Jehovah Rapha comes in, the God who heals.

> The thief's purpose is to steal and kill and destroy. My purpose is to give them a rich and satisfying life.
> —John 10:10 (NLT)

> . . . I am the LORD who heals you.
> —Exodus 15:26b (NLT)

God is the One who restores, mends, heals, and stitches us back together—Jehovah Rapha, the God who heals.

I have come to realize that to be mended, you must first be broken; to be stitched, you must first be torn or cut. Words can cut us deep, both those words spoken and the ones never spoken. Jesus knew we would need healing, that our hearts and lives would be broken, torn, and in need of healing that only He could provide.

We need healing from all wounds—the ones from our own choices and the wounds inflicted upon us from the choices of others, leaving our hearts ripped, torn, broken, cracked, or left in pieces. Many times, we don't even realize that our hearts need mending because we've learned to live with the effects of the hurt. Other times, we minimize the pain, thinking, "So many others have it much worse than I do." Jesus heals all the hurts and wounds, because each injury is significant to the one who felt the pain.

In my story, I didn't even realize I had any tears or rips remaining in my heart until I started digging deeper with the Lord. Jesus said He came to heal the brokenhearted and those crushed in Spirit.

> The Spirit of the Sovereign Lord is upon me, for the Lord has anointed me to bring good news to the poor. He has sent me to comfort the brokenhearted and to proclaim that captives will be released and prisoners will be freed.
> —Isaiah 61:1 (NLT)

My life had some significant wounds from childhood, teenage years, and even from adulthood. God was calling me into a place where He would begin to be Jehovah Rapha to my heart and my body.

When God started speaking to me about His name, Jehovah Rapha, I was very physically ill. I had been to several doctors, and none had a definitive answer for what was going on. The answers they did have offered no solution of healing. Many studies have found that when our hearts are wounded, it weakens the immune system. Well, my immune system was barely functioning.

I had diagnoses of fibromyalgia, chronic fatigue, chronic Lyme disease, insomnia, irritable bowel syndrome, and so much more. I completed treatment after treatment, infusion after infusion, only to get sicker. I truly felt and thought I was dying. My diet was clean—I ate and avoided any foods with triggers that were found in the food sensitivity tests. After a year of intense treatment and thousands of dollars spent, outside of my insurance coverage, the doctors had no idea what to do next. They could not figure out why my body wouldn't heal, so they sent me to a genealogist to study my DNA. We did more tests, but still no inclination of why I wasn't healing. I was sicker than ever, and my only hope was Jesus. My faith was tired, maybe about as tired as my body was.

God had spoken to me that the trauma I had endured was making my body sick. None of the preachers that I followed or listened to were teaching that, but I knew His voice, and I knew what He had spoken.

What I had heard God speak to my heart was true. Wounds, pain, and trauma can, in fact, make the body sick. I began seeking the Lord to heal my heart and welcome Him into those deep, painful places. We'll talk about the memories later. I took God at

His words and prayed for healing in my body and heart. I found many scriptures on healing and prayed them over my body, and I had wonderful people who prayed alongside me.

One Sunday, I was invited to a church service to hear a guest preacher. I had never heard of her, but a friend heard her preaching the night before about trauma and how it can make the body sick. I knew the church she was speaking at was one I could trust, so I went. I was amazed at what she was preaching. It was as though God had been reading her sermon notes to me in our time together.

That morning, she asked the crowd to take the piece of paper in their seats if they needed healing for anything and write each sickness on the back of the sheet of paper. I took my paper out quickly; I had a lot of diagnoses that were "incurable" in the eyes of modern medicine. She asked for people who had not been there the night before and needed healing to stand up. As I shared earlier, the Lord had been speaking to me through numbers, especially the number 4 and 44. I was the 4th person she chose to be prayed for. My spirit knew something was going to happen, though I wasn't sure what. I felt like all the faith I had was merely a mustard seed, but that's all you need.

> "You don't have enough faith," Jesus told them. "I tell you the truth, if you had faith even as small as a mustard seed, you could say to this mountain, 'Move from here to there,' and it would move. Nothing would be impossible."
>
> —Matthew 17:20 (NLT)

I stood in front of her and handed her my paper. She began reading my very extensive list of sicknesses, viruses, and diseases, then said, "Trauma, trauma, trauma . . . all that you have listed is because of trauma." I agreed, as the Lord had told me the same thing. She then said, "God is going to heal you today."

I felt like I didn't have an ounce of faith left, though I had prayed and prayed and prayed. I believed God could heal me, but I had not experienced any healing and had only had gotten worse. As those thoughts were going through my mind, she said, "I have enough faith for you."

Tears filled my eyes. The Lord was seeing and speaking right to me. She laid hands on me and began to pray, and immediately I felt the presence of Holy Spirit rush through my body. The power of God surging through my body was like a river of peace and electricity at the same time. It was the River of God flowing through me!

She prayed for healing for very specific things—even things that I had forgotten to write down. As I stood there, I wanted to collapse, but it felt like my feet were bound by cement, and I was unable to move at all. I could not even shift a toe, yet there was a trembling inside my body through God's power and His authority over the broken heart and broken body.

After she finished praying, she said something like, "Okay, you're healed. Go take your seat," but I still could not move at all, which I told her. A side note—just a few days prior to this move of God, I had received a prophetic word that I would be like Moses and stand on holy ground. In that moment, I remembered that prophetic word and knew I was standing on holy ground.

She looked at me and said, "Have you ever made fun of anyone being prayed over or ministered to?" I said, "Absolutely not." Though I may not have understood or at some points disagreed, I would not make fun of anyone because if the move was of God, I would be mocking the Lord Himself. I knew enough not to mock what I didn't understand. She then faced the audience and said, "Never make fun of what you don't understand," and I knew that was the Lord. As a child, I was teased terribly, and her words felt like the Lord protecting me and healing me from the childhood wounds of being bullied and picked on.

She then turned to me and said, "I hear the Lord saying you used to be some kind of athlete, and sickness stole that from you?"

I smiled and said, "Yes, I was a runner and was training for a marathon. I got sick and never recovered."

"Well, God wants you to run. Go buy a new pair of running shoes." She then said, "You know what we're going to do next?"

I just smiled, and said, "Run?"

With an expectation in her eye, she said "Yes!"

She had to take me by the hand, and my feet still dragged. We walked a few steps and then ran across the front of the church. I could feel the grave clothes of sickness falling off my body.

A sweet lady came up to me when I got to my seat and said, "I want to buy you new running shoes." Before I was prayed for, I sowed financially into this ministry; I gave what God put on my heart. God gave me back a double portion, because the shoes the other lady purchased for me cost double what I had sown into the ministry. There is a spiritual force in sowing and reaping. Remember that as you sow your money into ministries, you sow your money into good soil.

Jehovah Rapha, the God who heals, truly does heal body, soul, and spirit. He wants to heal every piece of your heart and body.

I got home that afternoon from the church service, and my husband said, "Wow, your eyes look different!" I sat in tears and shared with him all that God had done in my body and heart. The reminder that I am God's child came flooding into me, and I could feel His tangible love over my heart.

God touched me that day. He brought healing to my body to help me carry on with the healing He was doing in my heart. I continued seeking Him in an even deeper capacity. His touch in my body gave my heart strength and courage as I reflected on the God who sees and cares for me.

> Thereafter, Hagar used another name to refer to the Lord, who had spoken to her. She said, "You are the God who sees me."
>
> —Genesis 16:13a (NLT)

He is Jehovah Rapha and will bring healing to me. He will do that for you too! You can trust Him. He told me once, "Beloved, My DNA is faithfulness. You can trust Me." And that is truth! All through scripture, we see that His faithfulness endures forever.

Jesus doesn't always take away circumstances that hurt or are hurting us. The pain inflicted is still there, but knowing Him gives us an anchor to cling to in the storms. He is an anchor that heals all wounds, and He undoes the work of the enemy. He can heal every wound, trauma, and pain—the ones from our own choices, the ones from the choices of others, and some just from the storms of life.

In Job, we read that Job's misery washed away from him like a river.

> You will forget your misery; it will be like water flowing away.
>
> —Job 11:16 (NLT)

When the Lord brings healing, even the memory of traumas can wash away from you like a river. I know this to be true. There were some memories that were so horrific, even the thought of them would make me tremble, but when Jesus touches those places with His healing and His peace, the pain is healed and those places in your heart and body are restored. The Lord has washed the misery, hurt, and even some of the memories away from my heart. Some of the memories were so awful, I asked Him to wash them away from me like He did for Job. I know he truly did this for me because I was once reading over a past message I had prepared to share with a group of ladies. A specific memory that I had written down to share I no longer remembered! The Lord had washed it away. If He can do that for me, He can and will do that for you.

The very name Rapha is derived from the Hebrew word *rophe,* which is the Hebrew word for doctor. Jehovah Rapha is the God who wants to heal, mend, stitch, and restore your life back together. He desires to bring healing to every place that needs peace. His peace is the only lasting peace; scripture calls it the peace that passes all understanding.

Below are a few of my favorite scriptures of healing and encouragement. I clung to these; they were a lifeline for my soul. Even after I was prayed for and received radical healing, I would daily read through them. I encourage you to write down the ones that stand out to you on a sticky note or index card and place them in areas you'll see daily, places where you can remind yourself of them. Add them to the notes in your phone so you can read them when your heart needs to be reminded of who He is, what He is capable of, and what He wants to do in your heart.

And the peace of God [that peace which reassures the heart, that peace] which transcends all understanding, [that peace which] stands guard over your hearts and your minds in Christ Jesus [is yours].
—Philippians 4:7 (AMP)

He will once again fill your mouth with laughter and your lips with shouts of joy.
—Job 8:21 (NLT)

And He (Jesus) said to her, "Daughter, your faith has made you well. Go in peace. Your suffering is over."
—Mark 5:34 (NLT)

May we shout for joy when we hear of your victory and raise a victory banner in the name of our God. May the Lord answer all your prayers. *(An important note—victory in this verse means deliverance; hence, aid, victory, prosperity, health.)*
—Psalms 20:5 (NLT)

Your victory brings him great honor, and you have clothed him with splendor and majesty. *(An important note—victory in this verse means deliverance; hence, aid, victory, prosperity, health.)*
—Psalms 21:5 (NLT)

When they are sick, lying upon their bed of suffering, God will restore them. He will raise them up again and restore them back to health.
—Psalms 41:3 (TPT)

"I sank beneath the waves, and the waters closed over me. Seaweed wrapped itself around my head. I sank down to the very roots of the mountains. I was imprisoned in the earth, whose gates lock shut forever. But you, O Lord my God, snatched me from the jaws of death! As my life was slipping away, I remembered the Lord. And my earnest prayer went out to you in your holy Temple."
—Jonah 2:5-7 (NLT)

He offers a resting place for me in his luxurious love. His tracks take me to an oasis of peace near the quiet brook of bliss. That's where **He restores and revives my life**. He opens before me the right path and leads me along in his footsteps of righteousness so that I can bring honor to his name.

—Psalms 23:2-3 (TPT)

He heals the brokenhearted and binds up their wounds [healing their pain and comforting their sorrow].

—Psalms 147:3 (AMP)

The Lord is close to the brokenhearted; he rescues those whose spirits are crushed.

—Psalms 34:18 (NLT)

Peace, I leave with you; My [perfect] peace I give to you; not as the world gives do I give to you. Do not let your heart be troubled, nor let it be afraid. [Let My perfect peace calm you in every circumstance and give you courage and strength for every challenge.]

—John 14:27 (AMP)

A joyful, cheerful heart brings healing to both body and soul. But the one whose heart is crushed struggles with sickness and depression.
—Proverbs 17:22 (TPT)

There are so many more, but this is just a few to start.

The body and the heart are directly linked to each other. I believe that Jesus desires to heal us body, heart, and soul. I want to encourage you, any area in your body that has sickness, speak out healing over your body. Read the word of God out loud over your heart and body, and don't stop asking for healing. Also, I want to encourage you to ask God if there is any place in your heart that needs His touch. Write down what He speaks to you, and apply His Word in those areas. I believe a huge healing balm over sickness is releasing forgiveness and judgments and renouncing lies. When we renounce and come out of agreement with the lies, the truth can begin to take root.

Chapter Nine
Going Back to Go Forward

"Beloved, I want you to go back that you may go forward."

We had moved from our home to the town where my dad lived so I could cultivate a relationship with him. We were renting our current home to some friends; the plan was to sell that house and live happily ever after in the new town. The stress of trying to sell one house while we were renovating another one was overwhelming, so renting was a good option. It also helped to offset the cost of the renovations. When we moved, we never anticipated moving back. I was comfortable, settling into our new home and town. I visited my dad nearly every day, and God brought us a wonderful community. It felt like we were thriving!

I started getting sick while we lived there. There was a beautiful miracle of finding my dad, and then there were truths that unfolded that were like thorns in my heart. One day the Lord spoke to me, "Beloved, I want you to go back that you may go forward."

Now when God spoke that to me, I thought He was talking about moving back to our original home or town. This would obviously impact my husband, too, so as I said yes to God, I also asked of Him, "Please speak that to Tim."

The move to my dad's town wasn't an easy one. We didn't hire movers, but we had the help of one wonderful friend who, on his day off, made the trek to help us move, load after load. The renovations were not as glamorous as I those I had seen on television. It was hard work, mentally and physically exhausting. We had put so much work and money into this new home, but I know God's voice. When I heard him, I was shocked, yet a piece of me was comforted at His request. After all the work we had done and were still doing, moving back to our original city would be a big undertaking.

Days went on, and God did speak to my husband. He brought up in casual conversation about how much he missed the town we previously lived in, and that maybe we needed to move back. Once again, I was shocked, though I knew I had heard God correctly.

This stirring to go back to our previous community was so strong. I would go on my lunch break and look at houses in the area, fully expecting to move to a new home, but that's not how it worked out. Through a series of situations that wasn't as clear as I had expected, God confirmed we were to move back to our previous home. I assumed that because we said yes to God, the process of moving back would be beautiful and joyous, but that wasn't the case. God didn't tell us that it would be easy.

When God speaks something to your heart, write it down and hold onto it. If it's truly from God, it will come to pass, and if not, it will fall to the ground. Our season in this town had yielded good fruit, my roots with my dad were deep. I went to my dad and shared with him what God had spoken to me and to Tim. It was important to me to receive his blessing (which he gave us). I know it was still hard for him, but he knew that God had spoken to us.

The day we moved back home, the first step in the door felt like God was saying, "Welcome home." It was as though our hearts took a deep breath of gratitude, and delight surrounded us. I felt such a joy and anticipation of what God was going to do. We ended the moving day around the table with food, laughter, tired bodies, and happy hearts.

Later, I realized that one yes to God was not just saying yes to moving back to our previous home—God wanted my yes to something much bigger. He would ask me to go back into my childhood for me to move forward. It wasn't long until God revealed the details of what He meant, and my answer was still yes.

God doesn't force His way into our hearts or demand we listen. He is gentle and kind. His words eventually spoke beyond my soul and gripped my spirit. They set me on a trajectory of going back into my childhood to begin a deeper healing of my heart, one that was in a much deeper capacity than I had experienced. I could feel Jesus pulling me to a place that, though it felt safe, made me tremble inside.

Triggers

A trigger is when a pain from the past is being touched in the present by a similar situation that causes a feeling, emotion, or reaction. I call them invitations from heaven for healing. When the pain that's in your heart is touched and felt, it's remembered deep in your soul and even your body. Your response to present circumstances is typically not just to what is currently happening, but what occurred in your past that was buried instead of processed, or minimized as insignificant.

When I began digging deeper in my heart, I had no idea what a trigger was. In our current day, it's talked about so frequently and freely, almost overused like it's normal. The thing is, we aren't meant to live triggered; that's not the abundant life. If your heart surrenders to Jesus, a trigger can be an invitation to dig deeper with Him so He can heal and remove the pain. You need to go to the root of why the trigger happened. Finding out why is important to your emotional, spiritual, and physical health.

Being triggered could be small and seem minute, or it could feel crippling, like with a panic or anxiety attack. It can be a response that's just not a normal response for you. One of my bigger trigger responses was a full-on, hyperventilating panic attack. Yet another one was a sharp word spoken, and another time it was rescheduling a lunch. Each one represented something happening in my heart that needed healing. No matter the size of the reaction, the response is where the current situation is touching buried pain. These reactions don't necessarily mean you lose your emotional composure, and people around you may not even know—but you know.

For me and for many whom I've ministered to, much of that pain began in childhood. I didn't realize that most of what I was experiencing was a result of painful events that happened to me as a little girl. I was able to cope so well that I would dismiss any kind of triggers as just needing to spend more time with Jesus, worship more, or read more scripture. Sometimes even the opposite, thinking I deserved that response, and so on. All negating the fact that there was something painful buried in my heart.

Chapter Ten
Healing vs Coping

After we were back in our home, a significant incident occurred. The trigger of the situation was so significant that it sent me spiraling inside. I had tried my best to process it, sharing with God how it made me feel and forgiving the individuals, but I just couldn't shake how I felt inside. I had sat with Jesus and spoke forgiveness out loud, after which I would typically notice a release. I had trusted friends that I processed with, yet it still hurt deeply, and when the person was close, my body would tremble inside. The strong, painful emotions seemed to be lying in wait, like a volcano waiting to erupt.

In the past when I had forgiven, it felt like a healing balm over my heart. But this time, it was different, and I couldn't understand why, nor could I shake it. I truly felt shaken to my core. No matter what I did—declaring scriptures over my heart, worshipping, praying, sharing with a safe friend—I was still shaken, and I knew this was a big deal.

With encouragement from my husband, I started therapy. It was virtual, which made me feel safe. After the first session, I told God it was a waste of my time, and I didn't want to continue. The techniques the therapist suggested I do were ones that I'd used when ministering to others—I had tried all of that and knew I needed more. At the guidance of Holy Spirit and encouragement of my husband, I tried again with someone new, and the next therapist was different! She was a Holy Spirit-filled woman who was gentle yet strong, bold yet compassionate.

When I poured out my heart about the incident for the second or third time, she said, "When are we going to quit dancing around this and go back to the root of what happened in your childhood?"

I looked up at the screen as tears filled my eyes and then rolled down my cheeks. She was right. She then gave me "homework" to go and process with God. She didn't just give me a quick "go and do this or that and you'll be good." She sent me to the One who had the solution.

That day, I opened my heart to God in a new way and shared in detail what had occurred. I was willing to go back to wherever He wanted to go.

I journaled: *Help me with this Lord. I don't want to be angry. I want to forgive and let it go.*

God responded to me: Dear one, it begins with healing and letting go of all hurts from (name removed for the sake of privacy). The healing from that will flow into every facet of your life. It will strengthen you and enable you. I know you feel like you're going backwards, but only healing by going back to the root will allow you to go forward.

God's voice to me gave me the strength to continue. My trigger happened when the incident reminded my entire being of very similar incidents that repeatedly occurred as a little girl. The person standing in front of me reminded me of the wounding I felt as a little girl, both in my body and heart. I addressed with God how I felt.

Out loud, I spoke over myself, "You are safe today. God's arms are around you." It was like heaven coated each word and weaved a healing balm into my soul. Immediately, Holy Spirit gave me the following vision:

I was there as an adult, but seeing me as a little girl standing in front of a beautiful arched doorway. In the doorway was darkness and pain; it was covered by the black shadows. I saw the person who had first hurt me. They stood there looking at me as a little girl, and I took in how they were so massive, and I was so small.

With the guidance of Holy Spirit, I spoke to myself as a child and said, "You are safe today. God's arms are around you." The darkness evaporated, and light came in. The person that was so massively in my eyes disappeared, and as I stepped forward, the little girl disappeared. Through the power of Holy Spirit, I had faced the pain and hurt that was blocking me from stepping forward. God validated what I was feeling. His voice encouraged my heart, and His presence gave me boldness and courage.

The next steps for me would be processing through forgiveness.

> "You're not going to cope anymore. You're going to heal."

> I have told you these things, so that in Me you may have [perfect] peace. In the world you have tribulation *and* distress *and* suffering, but be courageous [be confident, be undaunted, be filled with joy]; I have overcome the world." [My conquest is accomplished, My victory abiding.]
> —John 16:33 (AMP)

Life is hard and pain is real. I believe that every person needs healing. Your life might be like mine or completely opposite, but one thing is for sure—we all experience hurt, pain, suffering, and loss. We will face many trials and sorrows. Life happens, and it can be devastating, but we can still experience peace, even in the breaking.

Most of what I had experienced was beyond hardships and fell under abuse. I needed an answer. One day, in conversation with God about some of the evil I had endured, I asked, "God, I know You are good. I know Your nature towards me is good. I don't know why bad things happened to me, but I know You. Why do bad things happen?"

Ever so gently, He replied, "Beloved, I give all humanity free will. It's a gift from Me. Some will use their free will for amazing and good things, and some will use it for evil. I knew that, so I sent My best, My Son, to undo the works of evil and bring healing to My children."

God gifted us with something wonderful—free will. He loves us deeply and desires wholeness for us. Jesus destroys the works of evil.

> For I know the thoughts that I think toward you, says the Lord, thoughts of peace and not of evil, to give you a future and a hope.
> —Jeremiah 29:11 (NKJV)

Evil and other bad things do not come from God because He is good. Jesus came to save the world. The word saved in Greek is *sozo*, meaning to make whole, to deliver, heal, keep safe, to heal one suffering from disease, to save. Jesus came to give life abundant and to save—to make humanity whole, deliver us, and give us a safe place in Him.

Pain happens in so many ways, like a parent walking away when they should have stayed or a loved one dying way before their expected time. Maybe you were bullied in school, you feel like you just don't fit in with your family, or it seems like your sibling is more loved than you. Perhaps your parents were excellent financial providers but emotionally shut off. We are in a broken world, a world where relationships can be complicated, some estranged. My heart is for you to welcome the Spirit of God into your heart where brokenness is (and could even be hiding) to let Him shine His light on those areas and bring full healing to your heart, body, soul, and spirit.

I know the power of Jesus to heal and restore. I also know it's a process; it's not a sprint but more like a marathon. Jesus is the only One who can set the captive free and give lasting freedom and healing. He can take the vilest sinner or the one who is broken and traumatized and turn them into a saint. He can take the deepest, darkest, most painful wound and heal it in such a way that even the scar is removed. I know this to be true. If He can and has done it for me, He can and will do it for you.

> . . . he will give a crown of beauty for ashes, a joyous blessing instead of mourning, festive praise instead of despair.

A sweet lady who had ministered to me reached out to check on me. I felt like I had opened a can of worms, and I just needed to figure out how to cope again. Her words "You're not going to cope anymore. You're going to heal" struck me to my core, cutting me to my soul, and that's exactly what I needed. God was done with me coping—we were going to dive into healing.

A situation once occurred in my life that hurt so deeply, I was sure I couldn't get through it or release it. The strong feelings lurked in the shadows, waiting to come out at any time, usually through sobs. I was stuffing down the pain and the powerful emotions. I later realized that was me just coping. We are not meant to live life coping. There are times where we must do so to survive in the short-term, but we aren't meant to remain this way. We are meant to heal. Jesus said He came to bring healing to the brokenhearted (see Isaiah 61:1-3) that we may live the abundant life.

> I came that they may have *and* enjoy life, and have it in abundance [to the full, till it overflows].
> —John 10:10b (AMP)

I didn't know it at the time, but the pain from the situation that day as an adult touched pain that originated all the way back in my early childhood. I truly thought that my heart was fully healed. After all, I could share in private conversations and on the stage about the terrible traumas I had endured, how Jesus had enabled me to forgive, all without crying. I thought *that* meant I was healed. I had received a lot of healing from Jesus, but there was more—a lot more.

There were other signs that showed I wasn't fully healed. At times, I could be very easily offended. I felt like I needed to be the best at everything I did. I don't mean just working with excellence—I mean that even when I received the utmost praise, underneath the smile, I felt like I could have done more or been better. I also sometimes believed that if I wanted something done right, I needed to just do it myself. I had an inability to rest and often overreacted. My home needed to be perfect... my *life* needed to look perfect.

As long as I could control what was happening around me, life was good. But when something happened that was outside of my control, I struggled to fully trust God. It was overwhelming. And this was all because I had merely been coping. I could encourage others to trust God, but when the buried pain inside was touched, it felt like more than I could take.

I *had* forgiven those who hurt me in childhood—and even in adulthood—and I could feel a level of healing, but also that there was more needed. The absence of complete peace was evidence of that. The Bible says we aren't just to have a visitation of peace but a habituation of peace.

> And the effect of righteousness will be peace [internal and external], and the result of righteousness will be quietness and confident trust forever. My people shall dwell in a peaceable habitation, in safe dwellings, and in quiet resting-places.
> —Isaiah 32:17-18 (AMPC)

Little by little, Jesus began drawing me closer and closer to His heart. He was inviting me to come and go with Him to a deeper place. He gently showed me where healing was needed, though it did not feel so gentle at the time.

I believe if we are going to know God on a deeper level, we must invite Holy Spirit in to dig deep into our own hearts. To ask Him to uncover the parts that hold pain. Our prayers must be real and honest about what we are feeling and experiencing. Many people pray simple prayers that are repetitive and could be said without any thought from our hearts. If we are going to go deeper with Jesus, then prayers need to be real and even raw. The conversation we have with God needs to reflect what's going on inside our hearts. If you ask Him to reveal what's hidden in your heart, He will.

> God, I invite your searching gaze into my heart. Examine me through and through; find out everything that may be hidden within me. Put me to the test and sift through all my anxious cares. See if there is any path of pain I'm walking on, and lead me back to your glorious, everlasting way—the path that brings me back to you.
>
> —Psalms 139:23-24 (TPT)

In the Bible, when David penned those words, he was inviting God to see if there was any pain in his heart. In the original Hebrew text, it talks about sorrow—"Search me O Lord, see if there is any pain or sorrow in my heart." It was an honest and real prayer. A prayer that is still in need of being prayed today.

Getting real and honest with God welcomes Him to touch the places of pain or sorrow in our hearts that have been buried deep. We must stop pretending that everything is fine and good when inside we feel fragile like a broken glass being held together with tape. If we say we've forgiven someone, but we go out of our way to avoid them, or the feelings that surface in our hearts when we think of them isn't honoring them or honoring God, then forgiveness isn't complete. A phrase I often hear is, "I have forgiven them, but I won't forget what they've done." These are all symptoms or signs that there is something deeper going on.

We aren't called to just be okay, to just cope. Each of us have a very specific call on our lives, and to complete that, we need to be the best version of ourselves. The death and resurrection of Jesus empowers that change. To walk in our calling, we must first know our identity, and to know our identity, we need to be healed. Healing opens the door to a life of peace and joy, a life where we're able to hear the Father's heart and experience Him.

In Psalms 34:8 the psalmist David calls us to taste and see, to come and experience His goodness.

> Taste and see that the Lord is good. Oh, the joys of those who take refuge in him!
> —Psalms 34:8 (NLT)

My hope is that the words I share in this book will bless you and lead you into newfound freedoms and full healing in Jesus. That you will gain the tools to be able to not only heal from past hurts but be able to reconcile your hurts and heart to Jesus. That you feel the depth of the Father's love for you.

May Holy Spirit wrap your heart in peace and give you strength to go to the places that are tender or painful to receive His touch.

And may you have the power to understand, as all God's people should, how wide, how long, how high, and how deep his love is.

May you experience the love of Christ, though it is too great to understand fully. Then you will be made complete with all the fullness of life and power that comes from God.

> Now all glory to God, who is able, through his mighty power at work within us, to accomplish infinitely more than we might ask or think.
> —Ephesians 3:18-20 (NLT)

PROMPT:

Choose today to open your heart up to God, to allow Him to touch places that haven't been touched in a long time.

Encouraged prayer:

Jesus, I come to You now. I ask for Your Spirit to come and move in my heart. Bring to the surface all You want to heal. I ask to feel Your lovingkindness over my heart and soul. I welcome You to come and have Your way in my life. In Your name, amen.

Chapter Eleven
Opening the Heart

Opening your heart to God is a daily choice.

REMEMBER THE PSALMIST DAVID's beautiful words in the Bible I mentioned above from Psalms 139:23-24. "God, I invite Your searching gaze into my heart . . . see if there is any path of pain, I am walking on . . ." David was opening his heart up to God.

I have prayed that prayer over and over: "Lord, search my heart and see if there is pain there. I open my heart up to You to bring healing." It's not just a one-time prayer but one to be given repeatedly.

As I've shared before, we are made up of four parts:

Spirit—made in the image of God
Body—our body
Soul—our mind (how we think), our will (what we want), and emotions (how we feel)
Heart—the seat of our being

When we accept Jesus, welcoming Him into our lives, the New Testament in the Bible calls it being reborn or born again. We still have our same body and soul, but our spirits become alive, activated, or reborn. We now have Holy Spirit to guide and lead us, help us on our journey. The things that don't instantly change are our souls, minds, wills, and emotions. In life, from childhood to current day, much of the wounding occurs in our souls, though I also believe the wounding, especially in cases of abuse, can go much deeper and wound our spirits. Many people don't realize that their souls and their hearts need healing.

Our Spirits are made in God's image; our souls are not.

> So, God created human beings in His own image. In the image of God He created them; male and female he created them.
>
> —Genesis 1:27 (NLT)

Hurts from childhood and life need to be repaired because they will have a deep effect on our souls. I knew this all too well. Just like a broken arm may need a cast or surgery, so it is with our souls. Healing the heart isn't just for those who have had traumatic childhoods—everyone needs healing. Maybe you even relate to my story of emotional, physical, and sexual abuse.

The truth is, we all experience pain and hurt. We live in a broken world; there's no way to avoid it. Someone passes away before you expected, a tragedy happens, you're betrayed by your best friend, changed schools as a child and lost your best friend, you had a car accident that changed your life, or a spouse passed away or asked for a divorce. Kids move on to college or start their lives and now it's just you or you and your spouse, you lost your job, you had to file for bankruptcy . . . there are thousands of scenarios. Yet one thing is the same—each of those situations hurt. There are all types and sizes, if you will, of wounding, but the answer is the same for each one of them: Jesus, the kind guardian who lovingly watches over our souls.

> . . . but now you have returned to the true Shepherd of your lives—the kind Guardian who lovingly watches over your souls.
> —1 Peter 2:25 (TPT)

In many churches, the topic of healing your heart is missing. Preaching on forgiveness is released, but not always what that forgiveness looks like, or even how to process through the pain that remains. Healing our hearts is needed in order to walk in wholeness. When you begin to let Jesus into the real and painful places, He begins to heal. A healed heart can receive the love of God; the opposite is also true. An unhealed heart cannot fully receive the love of God. You can be in church Sunday morning and then yelling at your kids or spouse on the way home.

Once we begin the journey of going back so that we can go forward, our hearts begin to heal, and we can start feeling the love of God. Once our hearts start healing, we then begin to truly know our identity—not just as God's child, but who we relate to in the Bible.

The next step is our calling and purpose. Many times, we get that mixed up and think we accepted Jesus and our identity is we're God's child, so let's get busy in our calling. But if your heart isn't healed and you try to step into your calling and purpose, you'll try to work *for* God's approval, not *from* His approval. You'll work trying to earn something that has been freely given.

In the Bible, we read that before Jesus had even stepped into ministry, before one miracle had ever been done, God the Father affirmed Him. Affirmation is a very real emotional need in all stages of life. God the Father spoke out how He was well-pleased and delighted. Like Jesus, we don't work for God's love and affection—we have it already.

> After Jesus was baptized, He came up immediately out of the water; and behold, the heavens were opened, and he (John) saw the Spirit of God descending as a dove and lighting on Him (Jesus), and behold, a voice from heaven said, "This is My beloved Son, in whom I am well-pleased and delighted!"
> —Matthew 3:16-17 (AMP)

When we open our hearts to healing, we can hear the voice of God our Father more clearly. When there is wounding and pain in our hearts, it makes it difficult for us to be able hear the voice of God and receive His love. The space in our hearts are taken up by wounds and we are unable to receive the love of God in those places.

Memory

It was around Christmas time, and we were gathering as a family. Everything was great as laughter filled the room . . . and then something happened. The incident that occurred would have hurt the feelings of most anyone, but it was a big trigger for me. The pain in the moment touched the core of my being, rushing in like a tidal wave. Immediately, I felt rejection and abandonment all the way back to the original place of pain—childhood.

I was feeling the pain from the incident combined with the pain from when I was a little girl. I got up and walked into the kitchen, trying to catch my breath and act like I was fine. For years, all the pain and trauma was swept neatly under the rug; it was how we coped. We didn't dare talk about it. Maybe because there was no answer, no resolution? It was so incredibly hard to process and, eventually, I would shut down and close that part of my heart off until it was touched by Jesus. He wanted me to face the pain of what happened and let Him bring healing.

I would need to face the strong feelings of being overlooked and flat-out rejected. Feelings that had fed lies that I wasn't just not good enough, but unlovable, and each lie would need to be uncovered and acknowledged.

For the truth to set you free, you must first realize you have been bound by the lies.

Healing and facing the pain is hard business, but the joy and peace that comes when it's removed truly brings God's glory, a peace that passes all understanding, the epitome of shalom. It affects the whole person.

Stones

When we have been hurt, the pains that sit in our hearts are like stones. The stones take up space where the love of God is supposed to consume, making it difficult to fully receive God's love. God confirmed this for me one day when my granddaughter had drawn me a picture. It was a heart will lots of little circles inside of it. They were colored in with ink, making them appear black they looked like stones.

In Ezekiel 36:26, the Bible talks about a heart of stone. I always thought that verse meant that before I received Jesus in my heart, that it was fully stone, becoming flesh afterward. But when I looked up the word *stone* in that verse in the original language of Hebrew, I learned that the stone can be large or small, it can be a weight, stone-like objects. It's not a heart that is fully stone, but a heart that has many or several stones.

When I started researching heart in this verse, I found it meant the inner man, our hearts, the seat of our emotions. When we are wounded, our emotions are wounded. When our hearts begin healing, the stones are removed, and we can receive the full love of God. Even our emotions begin to heal, and we become steadied.

Vision

One day as I was processing something painful, I spoke out loud what had happened and the pain I was feeling. God have me a vision.

I saw my heart as a garden and the pain as a stone. The stone was covered in bright, green, soft, beautiful moss—it had been in my heart so long that moss was growing over it! But under that moss was a hard, cold stone. The soil under it, though rich in nutrients from spending time with God, worship, and reading the word, could not grow a harvest because of the pain sitting on top of it. The stone was taking up the space where good things need to grow.

That's what pain, wounds, and hurts do in our hearts. We can spend time in the word, going to church, worshipping, memorizing scripture, etc., but the pain will take up the space where good seeds are supposed to grow. What God wants to plant can't be planted because the stones are consuming space in our hearts. God wants to give us a harvest that spurs us into our callings and purpose, but first we need to deal with the painful stuff.

I began dealing with the pain of not only that stone, but many others. I had struggled with overwhelming fear and what-ifs that could happen. If a certain memory popped up or I saw one of the men who had severely hurt me, the pounding in my heart would feel as though I was having a heart attack. I would say that I was healed because I had forgiven. I was able to pray blessings over the men who had hurt me so badly, and I could pray over others who had injured me. I thought because I could share my story of what had happened in my life without tears, but share it in faith and assurance, that I was fully healed.

Like I've said before, that's not real healing—that's coping, and it's spiritualizing away the pain, ignoring the pain to declare the good. But part of why Jesus died was so our pain could be healed.

My stones were of different sizes. Processing through sexual abuse was much different than processing through church hurt, yet each stone needed to be processed and healed. Holy Spirit began highlighting the stones, as if He had a flashlight in my heart.

I began to recognize stones quickly, like the one of someone in the church who had hurt me deeply. I realized I needed to process that stone with the Lord when I saw them at the grocery store and wanted to go in the other direction to avoid them. My behavior helped determine the next stone I needed to process.

This is part of the process and journey that God calls us to. To open our hearts in vulnerability and honesty to the One who can do something about the wounding in our hearts. God desires our most honest and vulnerable prayers. He truly is the One we can run to in safety, the One where our souls can hide until the storms pass. With Him we aren't just talking about what happened to us, we are inviting Him into the space where He can begin bandaging our wounds.

The Bible says that Jesus came to heal the brokenhearted and those crushed in Spirit.

> The Spirit of the Lord God is upon Me, Because the Lord has anointed *and* commissioned me To bring good news to the humble *and* afflicted; He has sent Me to bind up [the wounds of] the brokenhearted, To proclaim release [from confinement and condemnation] to the [physical and spiritual] captives And freedom to prisoners.
> —Isaiah 61:1 (AMP)

All of us, at some point or another, will have had our hearts broken; some of us have had this happen many times. Time doesn't heal all wounds. If wounds are left to time, they will develop infection that will look like bitterness, resentment, being guarded, easily offended, or unable to fully trust people or let them close. It can also cause us to pull people close just to push them away, struggle with anxiety and depression, fight feelings of rejection, or be unable to let go of offenses and more. This is evidence that the heart needs to be healed.

When we experience hurts, they create wounds in our souls. This can begin in childhood from our mom or dad (often unintentional), from people at school or church, our best friend who betrayed us, or disappointment from someone who let us down. Jesus came to heal those wounds; we aren't meant to just push them down.

At the time those feelings occur, we often don't know what to do with them or how to process them, so we bury them because the emotions are too painful. However, the feelings stay very much alive, and they next time you experience a similar wounding, the emotions will be compounded.

Healing our souls begins with being honest with the Lord about what we are feeling, going through, and have gone through. We tend to just push it down and keep going. We want to move away from coping to being healed, and in that healing, gain principles to help us remain in healing.

Chapter Twelve

Forgiveness

> But instead be kind and affectionate toward one another. Has God graciously forgiven you? Then graciously forgive one another in the depths of Christ's love.
>
> —Ephesians 4:32 (TPT)

> Later Peter approached Jesus and said, "How many times do I have to forgive my fellow believer who keeps offending me? Seven times?"
>
> Jesus answered, "Not seven times, Peter, but seventy times seven times!"
>
> —Matthew 18:21-22 (TPT)

FORGIVENESS IS ONE OF the biggest keys to walking in healing and wholeness. I do not believe we can walk in wholeness, be spiritually mature, or live the abundant life without forgiveness.

A root of bitterness will spring up, and its toxicity will flow into every relationship and facet of our lives. I learned early in my walk with the Lord that forgiveness was a big deal. I had experienced the freedom that forgiving someone brought.

Forgiveness is not a feeling but a choice, an act of obedience. I knew the Bible said we must forgive, and I was quick to forgive when someone hurt me, but it was easier to forgive a stranger than someone I loved, especially when the person who hurt me called themself a Christian. But we see in Matthew 18:21-22 that the scriptures refer to our fellow believer and can be translated as blood brother/sister or Christian brother/sister.

We are called to forgive, not seven times, but seventy times seven. When you forgive someone, especially in the situations of abuse, it's not letting them off the hook for what they've done. There are consequences for our choices. God is just and will deal with sins according to His wisdom.

Another misconception is, "If I forgive them, it means I have to be reconciled to them, and I don't know if I'm ready." Forgiveness doesn't always mean reconciliation to the person, but it does equal peace and our hearts reconciled to God, and He doesn't ask us to reconcile just to be hurt and or abused again. There is wisdom needed in rebuilding relationships.

In 1 Samuel 26, we read about how David had the opportunity to take Saul's life but didn't. He took his spear, and then when he was a safe distance away, he yelled back so that Saul would realize he had the spear. Saul repented and said that he wouldn't harm David, even asking David to come back with him. However, he did not return with Saul. Just because we forgive someone doesn't mean that we are reconciled to a relationship with them. But most importantly, our heart is reconciled to God.

One of the changes in forgiving that I implemented was not just praying "Lord, I choose to forgive them," but breaking it down into individual situations, individual stones, acknowledging the pain that was done to me per incident until it was released. One day, God spoke to me, "Beloved, forgive them, release them, then come and sit with Me." That statement from God wasn't an assignment just for that day, but for the rest of my life.

> Forgive them.
> Release them, the pain, the sin.
> Sit with Me.

That process brought breakthrough; there were some moments when I could physically feel the release from my body. Sitting with Jesus after a choice was made to forgive and release enabled me to pause and receive the love of God.

For if you forgive others their trespasses [their reckless and willful sins], your heavenly Father will also forgive you.

> But if you do not forgive others [nurturing your hurt and anger with the result that it interferes with your relationship with God], then your Father will not forgive your trespasses.
>
> —Matthew 6:14-15 (AMP)

We read in the above passages that if we do not forgive, what we are doing is nurturing hurt and anger, which interferes with our relationship with God and others. It also keeps our sins from being forgiven. Jesus said to forgive as you've been forgiven. Nurturing the pain or sin that was done to us or to someone we love doesn't bring healing, but is like allowing infection in a wound.

When we forgive, we are saying that the blood of Jesus is enough to cover their sins against us. It is not letting the person off the hook—it is saying we release them and what they did to hurt us to God. He is now responsible for them. We're coming into agreement with heaven that the blood of Jesus is enough to cover their sins.

I processed through forgiveness with this prayer something like this:

*Jesus, help me to forgive. I need Your help. I choose to forgive (**their name**) for what they did (**I spoke what they did to me**). Lord, it made me feel (**and spoke out every feeling that came to mind**). Lord, I choose now to forgive them. I release them to You; I release the sin they did and the pain it caused. All of it, I release to You. In Your name, Jesus, I pray. Amen.*

Even if you pray that prayer and feel nothing, if your heart meant it, there is an exchange God made. God takes your un-forgiveness and gives you back beauty for the ashes of pain.

There was a season when I was working through some deeply buried pain. During that time as I was healing, I took a sabbatical away from people who had hurt me. I set boundaries to guard my heart and protect the work God was doing. I desired reconciliation but knew I needed space for my heart to heal. That boundary I set, along with forgiveness, gave my heart the space it needed, and what came from that guidance of Holy Spirit brought good fruit, peace, and compassion.

Boundaries are meant to be like fences with gates. You cannot have boundaries without forgiveness, because what you will build aren't boundaries at all, but walls. The walls will keep the bad out, but it will also keep the good out and will bring emotional isolation. We cannot heal in isolation; we need safe people—community, friends, and family—to heal. We are built for community, but first we must heal, we must choose to forgive. That forgiveness, when partnered with boundaries, brings good.

An example of my boundaries was shortened phone calls. I would set timers of 10-15 minutes. If I was tired or stressed, I wouldn't have calls with that person until my heart was steadied. This boundary meant honoring my *no* and not giving in just to please the other person.

Story About Forgiveness

I want to share a story about forgiving. Soon after I had become a Christian (just a few weeks old in Christ), I called my mom and she told me, "I just want to let you know that Bob is dead." Bob was not his real name, of course. He was a man who had significantly abused me, even paying money to abuse me when I was a young girl.

Bob had apparently burned alive in his house; he was drunk and feel asleep with a cigarette burning. Instantly, Holy Spirit spoke to me, "Do not rejoice, for what he had to face was worse than anything you could imagine." The weight of those words took my breath. I knew it was not a time to celebrate that "he got what he deserved," but a time of solace, an awareness that God is just and is very aware of all that's happened to me. At that point in my walk with Jesus, I didn't know anything at all about healing or forgiveness besides that the Bible said to do so.

Many years later, I had become friends with a woman at my job. God told me He wanted me to be her friend, but that proved difficult, as I truly had to work for her to trust me, even just a little. She was very closed off. I looked for opportunities to be kind to her, to say hello, going out of my way to find her. Finally, after about eight months, maybe even a year, I found something we could connect with, and it opened a door. She slowly began trust me and would pause to have conversation with me.

One day, I realized it had been a couple weeks since I had last seen her. Her schedule was different that mine, and depending on how her days off fell, several days could go by without me seeing her. I found out she had been diagnosed with cancer, and the diagnosis wasn't good. I was able to connect with her sister and scheduled a time I could visit.

I asked my friend, "What can I bring you? Anything—just name it," I was thinking I'd run out and grab whatever she needed. She replied, "A chilled pineapple upside down cake."

I had never even made a hot one, but I learned how real quick. My husband ate my first attempt . . . it wasn't exactly the best.

I baked her cake, let it cool, packed it on ice, and took off to see my friend. As I sat with her in her room, sometimes at her feet sharing stories, a deeper bond began to develop. Even typing this, tears fill my eyes, she became more that just my friend—she became my sister, and her family became my family. I found a space to open up and be vulnerable about things that honestly shocked me that I was sharing. Once I even said, "I have no idea why I just shared that." Her sister, who became so dear to my heart, said, "I know why. We have a similar thing that happened in my family, I needed to hear that." I loved this family.

One day at work, I received a call. My friend had passed away. I had firmly believed she would be healed, not in the eternal life, but on earth. It was like a kick in my gut. I had fully believed for her healing, and in the end, she was fully healed, just not in the way I expected or wanted. This beloved family honored me; I was asked to be a part of delivering her eulogy. I could not have been more honored if I had been speaking for the President of the United States.

I asked for the address of the church, and they texted it to me. When I read the address, my heart sank, and my breath seemed to be taken from me. It was the same town where I had been significantly abused. I knew God had given me the honor to go there, and He would give me the strength too.

While on my way to the church the morning of the celebration of life, Holy Spirit spoke to me, saying I needed to go back to where the abuse happened.

I delivered the message God gave me at my friend's celebration of life, and what an honor it was. The words that stood out to me from what God had spoken was "She was not justified in how she lived her life, but in Whom she believed in." She trusted Jesus and then met Him face to face. I believe He embraced her with a soft smile and gentle embrace.

I didn't tell anyone where I was going next out of fear someone would try to talk me out of going. I spoke with God then drove to the location. I couldn't find any resemblance of the house; I approached a bridge and realized I had gone too far, so I turned around and drove back.

When I told God I couldn't find the place, immediately He replied, "Look out the window." I did, and it was the location. God said, "See, even the land is different. I destroy everything that raises itself up against My children." There was an authority and loving sternness in His voice.

The weight of the revelation and His words were so heavy, the lump in my throat nearly choked me as the tears streamed down my face. God had seen the significant abuse; my cries of suffering had reached His ears. My pain cried out, demanding to be heard, and God heard, and He came.

Holy Spirit then said, "Now go to the other location." I knew He meant the house where the other man who had severely hurt me lived, the one that burned alive in his house. Just like before, I couldn't find the specific location and drove by it. I got to the post office and turned around and drove back. Immediately, God said, "Look out the window." Just like before, I knew it was the right location. God said, "See, I said I destroy everything that raises itself up against My children."

Forgiveness doesn't let someone off the hook; it accepts the blood of Jesus as payment for their sin and allows you to release them to God. Their sin then becomes the responsibility of God so we are no longer holding onto it, demanding someone pays. Jesus paid for their sin. When we forgive and release, the peace of God then has a place to reside in our hearts.

When we withhold forgiveness, it's like drinking poison and expecting it to hurt the other person. Beloved, it doesn't hurt them, it deeply hurts *us*. When we don't forgive, anger, hurt, and bitterness is buried in our hearts, and it will eventually come out.

If we don't forgive and release it, it comes out as outbursts of anger, rage, depression, overreaction, being easily offended, being negative, anxiety, the inability to trust others, and so on. Remember, it can even come out through exhaustion, fatigue, or sickness, sometimes sickness that is unexplainable or can't be diagnosed.

Un-forgiveness will destroy your heart and body from the inside out. Again, forgiveness isn't saying that what they did was okay or that there aren't consequences for their actions. Forgiveness also isn't minimizing what happened to you, especially in the incidence of abuse. It's about releasing the person to Jesus to remove the weight of their offense from your heart. It's replacing pain, hurt, anger, and bitterness with the peace of God. Forgiveness is exchanging the pain for peace. It's a simple choice that was paid for at a high price—Jesus died for us to be able to have that exchange.

Forgiveness isn't just for the really big things. It touches every aspect of our life. We need to stop minimizing and, instead, walk through forgiveness and how the hurt affected us. This is true even if we now deem the incident as small or insignificant, especially when compared to the pain or situations of others.

We forgive the friend who ended a friendship with no explanation, the boss who doesn't appreciate our work, the friend who betrayed us, or the parent who made significant mistakes. We forgive anything that stings our hearts and stirs emotion. At the slightest sting or offense in my heart, I am quick to pray through forgiveness, as I don't want anything planted in my heart that could negatively affect my relationship with God and others.

When I think of forgiveness, the imagery I see is like a finger with a small cut, like from gardening. You need to wash the cut, even if it's small, to avoid infection. It needs to be acknowledged and tended to; the cut may just need to be washed and have a bandage applied, or it may require going to a doctor and getting stitches.

Challenging situations are like that—when our hearts are hurt, it could be a quick forgiveness prayer and releasing the person, or it may need more attention, like prayer with a safe person or pastor. It might require you to pray and release the person 70 x 7 times. Whatever the situation, however the size, if it stirs your heart into anger or hurt, it's worth digging into.

When I started digging deep with what I was really feeling, all that I had buried for years, it was a lot to process. I ended up taking a working sabbatical—I know, an oxymoron. I still had to work because I had a full-time job, but I took a season off from ministry and from serving. I sat with the Lord several hours each day, separately from my God Time. I spoke out everything that had happened, writing letters of the painful situations and all the emotions, feeling them and releasing them. Giving voice and acknowledgment to the pain was like breaking off the hard shell around my heart so I could fully feel the love of God.

We not only need to forgive those who have hurt or wronged us; sometimes we need to also forgive ourselves, our mistakes or choices that hurt others. We hold the sin of un-forgiveness against ourselves when God is calling us to let us go, to let His mercy and grace be enough. You may need to forgive God, not because of anything He has done wrong. but because deep inside our hearts, there are times we hold Him responsible. I remember crying out, "God, You could have stopped that . . . You could have . . . ." My prayers pulled Him closer. His compassion seemed to engulf me as I yelled out at Him because He didn't do what I thought He should have. My raw honesty was met with a kindness that can only be explained by experience.

Forgiveness isn't always forgetting, either, though I have experienced memories being washed away. With other wounds, I can still remember what happened, sometimes in detail, but the remembrance no longer holds pain. The healing in our hearts cannot begin until we make the decision to forgive. We forgive so we can be free.

Forgiveness is between you and God, not you and the other person, and it doesn't equal reconciliation. We don't wait until we feel like it—we make a choice to forgive. We don't wait for the person who wronged us to apologize because that may not happen. In some cases where I have ministered, the person who hurt them was deceased and unable to ask for forgiveness. We must take the first step and decide to forgive. Otherwise, if we wait for the one who hurt us to apologize so we can forgive, we are placing our healing in the hands of the one who hurt us.

Our healing must be placed in God's hands; He wants your heart to be healed and whole, and forgiving tills the soil of your heart to receive good things. There may not be an immediate change in your feelings, but when we forgive, there is an exchange, and the peace of God will saturate our hearts.

PROMPT:

As you are reading this, if your heart has been stirred, I encourage you to make a choice to forgive from your heart. Even speaking it out loud as a declaration—"God, today I make a choice to forgive from my heart"—carries a weight and authority.

Start a list of everyone you can think of that's hurt you in any way. Even if you think you've already forgiven them, write down their name and what happened.

Next, invite Holy Spirit to come and reveal anyone you missed.

Simple Prayer:

Holy Spirit, I invite You to come and bring truth to my heart. Please bring to my remembrance anyone I need to forgive and the event that hurt me.

Once your list is complete, walk through forgiving each person for each offense. If you're like me and have a lot of names, don't skip any or race through them as quickly as possible. Take the time to process each one so you can release them and walk in peace. Don't rush this as just a check-off list, but spend time with Jesus in this. Don't pray a blanket prayer, but go through each one individually. You might need to break it up into more than one session. Take deep breaths and dive deep into the pain to receive the healing balm of Jesus over the wound.

Example prayers:

*God, I come to You now in the name of Jesus. I choose to forgive **(say their name)** and what they did **(speak out loud what they did or failed to do)**. Jesus, it made me feel **(speak out every feeling that comes to mind)**. What **(their name)** did to me was sin.*

*Jesus, right now I chose to accept Your blood as payment for their sin against me. I release the sin they did to me and the pain I feel. **(Take a few deep breaths, for me this is a prophetic act of receiving the fresh strength and peace of God and releasing the pain)***

Jesus, I choose to forgive them right now. They no longer owe me for what they've done. Jesus, I release this offense and pain to You. In Jesus' name, amen.

You may need to pray this prayer several times, beep making the choice to forgive, and the feelings will follow. This is a practice I still use in my life. It's a way of keeping my heart pure and helps me to walk in hand with Jesus.

Forgiveness can be hard, but the reward is peace.

> But instead be kind and affectionate toward one another. Has God graciously forgiven you? Then graciously forgive one another in the depths of Christ's love.
>
> —Ephesians 4:32 (TPT)

Then you will experience God's peace, which exceeds anything we can understand. His peace will guard your hearts and minds as you live in Christ Jesus.

—Philippians 4:7 (NLT)

Chapter Thirteen

Judgments

Judge not lest ye be judged.

"Do not judge others, and you will not be judged. For you will be treated as you treat others. The standard you use in judging is the standard by which you will be judged.
—Matthew 7:1-2 (NLT)

I HAD WORKED THROUGH so much forgiveness, saying yes to Jesus, that His blood was enough to pay the price for what others had done to me. I had a lot of breakthroughs!

But, in some areas, there was still pain that had a grip on my heart. Situations where I felt entitled to be angry—I was angry at who allowed me to be hurt, not just who hurt me. I had no idea I was actively judging those who had hurt me and had hurt those I love. Some of what I judged about the people who had hurt me didn't sound entirely bad. What I felt about them was true to me because I was judging was from a place of pain and hurt.

When we're hurt, especially as children, the natural response is to judge the one who hurt us. I wasn't judging the fruit in their lives or the sin done, but the person. I was raising myself above them, and I felt justified in doing so. The way I felt about them in my adulthood was the judgment I made about them in childhood. After all, I was the one hurt and, in many cases, severely abused. I had not done what they had, so I felt better than them, which is also pride.

God alone holds the place and right to judge, but I had taken God's place as judge in their lives. I wasn't just stating a fact of what they did. Deep down, my thoughts were, "How could you ever do something like that?" and "What kind of person are you?" and "If you had been here, this wouldn't have happened." These were thoughts engrained and wrapped with anger and hurt, the deep rooted pain fueling my judgments.

A visual I see is the painful act, the sin done to me, like the ingredients in a box of cake mix. Lots of factors (ingredients) all mixed. Then, a judgment was added—like adding water to the mix—and now it's not just ingredients, but it's activated.

> Look after each other so that none of you fails to receive the grace of God. Watch out that no poisonous root of bitterness grows up to trouble you, corrupting many.
> —Hebrews 12:15 (NLT)

Even as children, when we are hurt by someone we love—particularly our parents—the natural, humanistic response is to judge them for what they did or didn't do. Most children are unable to truly process the pain, and it gets buried in our hearts. Then as adults, when something similar happens and we have that trigger response, the judgment we made as children is brought back to the forefront of our heart and is spiritually activated in our lives.

As I began to dig deep into this spiritual principle, I could feel inside my heart that this revelation in the Word of God was true, and much of the pain I was experiencing was from judgments I made against people who hurt me. Even when we sow just a tiny judgment, what comes back is a whirlwind in our emotions and relationships.

> For they sow the wind [in evil]And they reap the whirlwind [in disaster] . . .
>
> —Hosea 8:7 (AMP)

When we judge, there is a principle that is released, and the power behind it will be unleashed in our lives. I believe this is why Jesus told us:

> "Do not judge others, and you will not be judged. For you will be treated as you treat others. The standard you use in judging is the standard by which you will be judged.
>
> —Matthew 7:1-2 (NLT)

For every action there is a consequence. Some are good and some are bad. When we judge from a place of pain, we will reap that pain until we repent of that sin. Again, it's not sin to state what happened or was done to us, but it is a sin to judge the person who hurt you (or allowed you to be hurt) from a place of pain. In God's Kingdom, we don't just get back what we sow—we get more. It's the law of increase. The longer a judgment sits and matures, the worse it's affected. Most of the time, the judgment we pronounce on the one who hurt us, especially our parents in childhood when we experienced the pain, was buried it, sometimes so deeply that we don't even remember it. As that judgment grows and matures, it will produce a harvest, but what is sown in the darkness will reap darkness back.

When I sat with Jesus and walked with Him through so much pain, I went through situations where I had released forgiveness. I humbly asked Holy Spirit to please remind me of any judgments, and they began slowly coming up. The judgments I had made didn't sound all that bad, but they were still judgments. In many of these, I felt so justified—that all I had experienced warranted a strong judgment. That sense of entitlement is a sign that there have been judgments made. When we do that, we put ourselves above another person, casting the judgment we think is appropriate. But we don't get to pick and choose who deserves grace and who doesn't because we are not the judge. Jesus is.

> And He (God the Father) has given Him (Jesus) authority to execute judgment, because He is a Son of Man [sinless humanity, qualifying Him to sit in judgment over mankind].
> —John 5:27 (AMP)

If we have judged, it creates a boomerang that will come back to us. Judge not lest you be judged. What it brings back is pain, disappointment, and fear, and many times, whatever we judged we will end up doing the same. We will do the very thing we judged our parents for. Or we will expect others to do the same thing to us that our parents did.

I remember the moment I saw my mom do something that she obviously did not mean for me to see. I was around 9 or 10 years old, and I recall thinking, "How could you do that? You're a terrible person." When I became an adult, the very sin I judged her for as a child, I committed, and the very sin I committed I then expected others to do to me.

When I received the revelation of judgments, especially from the verse in Hosea, I immediately prayed, "God, I realize in my pain that I judged my mom. Please forgive me for judging my mom for (here, I spoke out the incident). I repent for this sin. I ask You to put this sin to death on the cross, and I ask you to resurrect new life. May this sin not be held against me. I receive Your blood as payment for me judging her."

I asked for resurrected life in the area of my heart that once held the judgment. I no longer raised my heart above my mom's; I had repented for judging her and received the forgiveness of Jesus over my heart and life. Repentance brings humility and gives God the rightful place of releasing judgment. I am ever so thankful for the cross that brings mercy, grace, and forgiveness—it covers all sin. The power of the cross and resurrection of Jesus breaks the power of sin!

I shared earlier some of the horrific things I had endured. The abuse was significant and obviously not fair. The world isn't fair—we live in a fallen world—but we also cannot take on a victim mentality. Bad things were done to me, and I judged harshly these bad things, both in childhood and adulthood. Once I opened my heart to Jesus to first walk through forgiveness and then repent for judgments, He was able to do a major work in my heart.

One day, before I knew anything about judgments in this capacity, Jesus told me, "When you are feeling judgmental, turn to wonder. 'I wonder what they have been through to bring about that action?'" That question changed how I saw others and paved a way for me to begin to repent for judgments.

I had a season where I sat with the Lord. I analyzed every place that I still felt pain and asked Holy Spirit how I had judged the person. He revealed and I repented. Now I recognize judging others quickly and am quick to repent, and I don't wait for my God time to do so. I immediately stop what I'm doing and make space to repent out loud, asking the Lord to forgive me as I turn to wonder and pray for the person. This simple process changed my heart and life.

In the situations where I had forgiven but just could not get over or through it, there were judgments that I needed to repent. When I did that, the heaviness left my heart!

PROMPT:

Go back through your list from where you processed through forgiveness. If you don't have that list, Holy Spirit will remind you if you ask Him to bring to your mind each judgment you made from each place of hurt. Write down what you judged and then pray over each one individually. You may need to pray and release forgiveness again—if so, that's okay. Each person's timeline for healing is different.

*God, I come to You in the name of Jesus. I realize that from a place of pain, hurt, and anger. I have judged **(their name)** for **(what they did or didn't do)**. Today, Lord, I choose to forgive **(their name)** for **(what they did or didn't do)**.*

*God, I ask You to forgive me for judging them for **(what they did or didn't do)**. Right now, in the name of Jesus, I choose to release all pain, hurt, anger, and bitterness from my heart and body. I put to death these judgments on the cross, and I ask You to resurrect new life in me.*

I ask You to wash my heart clean, removing this now. I receive Your blood and payment for these sins. In Jesus' name, amen.

Chapter Fourteen
Processing Memories

The memories would be touched and healed.

When I received the word about what the number 44 meant in my life, I knew that God was going to take me deeper. It was not easy. As I began to process through so much of what had happened to me, the weight pressed down on me. I had forgiven those who had hurt me, and I felt the release of that both in my body and soul. I began repenting for judgments, but some of the memories were very heavy, specifically in the incidences of abuse.

> In Job, we read that Job's misery washed away from him like a river.
>
> You will forget your misery; it will be like water flowing away.
>
> —Job 11:16 (NLT)

When we invite the Lord to bring healing, even the memory of traumas can wash away from you like a river. I know this to be true. There were some memories that were so horrific, even the thought of them would make me tremble inside. I had buried the memories and just tried my best to forget about them. But when Jesus touches those places with His healing power and love, and His peace reaches where the pain is, there is a healing that comes to that place in your heart and body, and both are restored.

Blondie

I started a process long ago that I referred to as "counseling with Holy Spirit." God would sit with me as we walked through deep painful situations. Once when I was processing through forgiving, Jesus said, "Ask Me where I was." So I began welcoming Him into the memories, but this particular day was different. I wasn't sitting and processing with God; I was just sitting on the floor, going through some books, and the memory of how my dog Blondie had died came rushing to the front of my heart and mind.

I had processed through forgiving how the terrible event had happened, but there was more. I loved my dog. She was true to her name and blonde in color, and the texture of her hair was coarse. Blondie was a good dog, and with such a traumatic childhood, she was the kindness of God to me. As this memory came up, Holy Spirit spoke to me, "Beloved, invite Me into the memory." Even as I type this, I get chills.

I responded, "Jesus, come into this memory." It was as though I went back in time, inside that memory as a little girl—I must have been about 7 or 8 years old. Next, I watched the horrific scene of how she was killed. It wasn't only that she died, which was horrific enough, but the ache and hurt in my heart of knowing she went under the house and was alone. I couldn't hold her or comfort her as she took her last breaths.

In this vision, I watched Jesus go under the house. It was as though the house was translucent, and I was able to see clearly. I watched Blondie taking her last breaths, and I saw Jesus wrap Himself around her; He held her and comforted as only He could, as He was her creator. And Jesus was comforting me too, as He is the kind guardian who lovingly watches over our souls.

Because that memory held such pain, He went back into my childhood and gave me vision and sight. He touched and healed my heart. Jesus reframed the memory, changing the history I knew by showing me what had really happened, and the pain was released and removed, touched by God's kindness. Now that memory doesn't hold pain; it holds the kindness of Jesus, Who was willing to get in the dirt to hold His creation and to soothe His child. That is the Jesus who gave His life for the world.

Outside

I want to share one more story on processing memories. I have sat with Jesus through hundreds of memories, so the process was one that I was familiar with.

In this memory, I was around seven or eight years old. I was at my mom and stepfather's house in the summer, and it was hot outside. We lived in an area with high humidity, so the temperature could get about 95-98 degrees and could feel like 110. I'm not sure why, but my stepfather decided to lock me out of the house to make me go play.

I remembered banging on the door, begging to come inside until their response was harsh enough that the punishment for beating on the door outweighed the suffering of being outside. I'm not sure how long I was outside, overwhelmed by the heat. As I sat with Jesus in this memory, He said, "Ask Me where I was," so I did.

I saw Him walk up behind me, and His shadow brought an instant coolness. Then He took me to the corner of the porch, sat down with legs crossed, placed me in His lap, and shielded me from the sun. It was like sitting in a shade that shielded and replenished at the same time. He stayed here with me until the door was unlocked, and I was allowed back inside the house. Jehovah Rapha, the Lord who heals, mends, and stitches our hearts back together. He loves His children, His creation, and longs to heal what the enemy has tainted and tried to destroy.

Bathtub

When I was deep in my healing journey, one of the things I would do at the end of the day to try to help my body recover from what I was going through spiritually and emotionally was take hot Epsom salt baths. I added lavender and rosemary essential oils, and the water soothed and comforted both my body and soul.

One afternoon, I was in the water, crying to the Lord. The pain that was stuck in my soul was so intense that I couldn't tell if I was being tormented by Satan or if Jesus was at work healing. The sobs were so loud that I used a washcloth to muffle the sound. I cried out to Jesus, "Is this You or is Satan tormenting me?"

Immediately, the Spirit of God came and lifted me out of the water. I said, "No, I'm naked!" He then covered me with something like pure, white silk that draped over my body but didn't stick to my skin. He then laid me in the arms and lap of Jesus; God the Father pulled in close. God the Father, Son, and Holy Spirit wrapped around me, softening the sobs until they ceased, healing the pain. It was such a significant experience. When Holy Spirit then brought me back to the water, the water was cold.

I remember sitting in the water, astonished and amazed about what had happened. To this day, I'm still amazed at the kindness of God to the hurting. He does not abandon Hs children in their pain or ignore their suffering—it draws Him close. When, I was back in reality, awestruck, I whispered, "God, did that really happen?"

He told me to look at my feet, and there was a feather floating in the water. I took a picture to make sure I wasn't imagining it. The next night, a feather appeared again. Miracles, signs, and wonders will follow those who believe. God is close to the brokenhearted.

> The Lord is close to the brokenhearted; He rescues those whose spirits are crushed.
> —Psalms 34:18 (NLT)

> He will cover you with is feathers. He will shelter you with his wings. His faithful promises are your armor and protection.
>
> —Psalms 91:4 (NLT)

The Lord has washed the misery, hurt, and many of the memories away from my heart. I have sat with Him hour after hour, letting Him touch painful places to bring His soothing peace.

Some of the memories were beyond horrible, so I asked Him to please wash them away from me like He did for Job. I believe that when I didn't have the capacity to process them, and though I don't remember when or how, He did wash them away.

Remember that one day I was reading over a past message I had prepared to share with a group of ladies? I had written down a specific memory in my notes to share, but as I read back over it, I no longer remembered the memory! It was as though I was reading someone else's story. I knew it was true, but the Lord had washed the memory and the pain of it away. If He can do that for me, He can and will do that for you.

Working through painful memories brought not only peace but also comfort to my soul.

PROMPT:

When you have released forgiveness and repented for judgments but the memory still has pain, take that memory captive to the secret place with Jesus. Invite Him to the place where they reside, and ask Him to show you where He was. Welcome Him to the painful place. Let His presence soothe your heart and soul.

Don't be quick to dismiss a memory, even if you think it's too small or insignificant. Let Jesus minister and heal your heart.

Chapter Fifteen

Emotions and Emotional Needs

Emotional needs are to the soul what food and water are to the body.

I HAD MET JEHOVAH Rapha and experienced radial healing in my body, soul, and spirit. I worked through forgiveness and judgments, releasing the pain and people who had hurt me, bringing significant freedom and peace. And as I worked through painful memories, not just once I had finished processing, God brought a deep peace and comfort to me. These processes allowed painful places to be tenderly touched by His love.

As I shared in the beginning, my life looked great on the outside, and many parts of it were. I was anointed to preach and teach and was able to flow in that gifting. People were being touched by God's love, but I was being depleted in a significant way. I was bubbly, friendly, kind, and generous, and I truly loved people. I was teaching, ministering to others, and leading an intercessory prayer team, but I would walk away feeling so incredibly drained, and it would take days to recover from what I had poured out.

I resided in performance, waiting on the applause of man to confirm that I did well. I would continually overthink: did I share too much, or did I not share enough? Was what I brought too heavy, or was it too light? Would people still like me or think differently about me?

I was so caught up in needing affirmation from people that I was unable to receive or hear the applause of Heaven. Deep inside, I knew there had to be more, because surely this wasn't the abundant life Jesus talked about.

> I came that they may have *and* enjoy life, and have it in abundance [to the full, till it overflows].
> —John 10:10b (AMP)

It was as though no matter how hard I tried, there were "fruits" in my life that I couldn't overcome. I couldn't seem to stop wanting to control things in my life, which meant I wasn't able to trust God fully. I didn't want to be overcome with perfectionism and obsessive-compulsive disorder—I wanted all fear to leave, to be able to lay my burdens on the altar and not pick them back up. I wanted to be able to trust that God was going to come through for me, that He was truly going to fight for me, not just for everyone else. I had no idea that much of what I was dealing with was a result of unmet emotional needs until God brought me to a place to receive revelation.

One night I had a dream where I was standing in the center of a room near a faucet, and this bright, light blue water was pouring from it. Six people stood to my left, staring at me. I was then on my knees, crying, and I said, "I just can't get to the living water." I was painfully aware of the desperation in my heart.

I woke up, still feeling the weight of it. I knew this dream was from God. That morning, I reached out to a friend who thought I possibly needed to go to a retreat at Living Waters Ministry. I was reluctant and replied that I didn't know those people and couldn't afford to let anything get planted in my heart that wasn't from the Lord. During this time, I was stuck emotionally in a particular situation, one that drew me to therapy for the first time in my life.

I searched online to get information on Living Waters Ministry; I knew my dream was significant. That morning, I heard two teachings. The first teaching was "Stony Heart," and the second one was "The River of God." As I analyzed the teachings, I couldn't find anything that wasn't in alignment with scripture. That afternoon, I had a virtual session with my therapist. She was an amazing, spirit-filled woman of God, and at the end of our session, she said, "I hear the spirit of God saying that you have a stony heart and that you need the living water."

I almost fell out of my chair. I sat in sobs; I knew that God was speaking to me. I can't remember if it was that day or the next, but I contacted Living Waters Ministry and went to my first retreat. It overwhelmed my heart. I had no idea that there were wounded places remaining, and I had no idea about the unmet emotional needs. That revelation changed my life.

When this revelation came, it made sense why I couldn't put myself into the fruit of the spirit, couldn't make myself have more patience or self-control. But once I began processing what I'm getting ready to share, the fruit of the spirit began flowing from me before I even realized it.

Early in the church, I was taught to stay away from feelings because they would lead you away from God and couldn't be trusted. I remember hearing and even saying things like, "Faith over feelings." We looked only to faith, and our feelings were treated like something bad, something to be dismissed or overcome. Feelings couldn't be trusted, so they needed to be ignored.

After being baptized with Holy Spirit, I felt God lead me to read the scriptures and let Him speak to me, As I read the Bible through a fresh lens, especially the New Testament, I quickly realized it was full of Jesus showing and bringing attention to emotions. I read how Jesus was moved with compassion and deep sorrow as He wept over His friend Lazarus. He was acquainted with grief, sorrow, and anger, even displaying the latter in the Temple.

Jesus didn't dismiss emotions; He felt them *deeply*. I began to realize that emotions weren't something to be pushed down or pushed away, but they are to be felt and brought to Jesus to welcome Him into them. Emotions are an indicator that something is happening in our hearts.

Our emotions are like the indicator lights on our car's dashboard, and our hearts are the car. When a light comes on, it's an indicator that something about the car needs attention. Not necessarily anything bad—an indicator light could be time to change the oil or that a tire needs air. Feelings, our emotions, can be a powerful sign that something is going on beneath the surface. An indicator that something inside our heart and soul needs attention. If ignored too long, the result can be bad.

As an example, if the indicator to change your oil comes on and you fail to take care of it, the result could be serious damage to your car's engine. The same is true when we ignore our emotions. I believe emotions are a gift from God. They also can be greatly wounded, and that's where we can get led astray. Jesus and only Jesus can truly heal them and fulfill the emotional needs that we have.

When we take the time to listen, feel, and understand what our emotions are pointing to, processing them with Holy Spirit, the result is powerful and brings healing, understanding, and revelation to the deep places in our hearts. When we tend to our emotions, we can then begin to grow into maturity. Our hearts *need* consistency and unconditional love.

Emotional Needs in Childhood

When our emotional needs as children are not met, the evidence can be seen in adulthood. What I thought was a need to "just act better" was the result of emotional needs not being met in my childhood. But no childhood is perfect—even the best parents cannot fully fill these needs.

Emotional needs are to be fulfilled through God's original design, our biological mother and father. If a parent is missing, there is an automatic depletion. In the situation of adoption, there is still a depletion, even with the most loving and caring adoptive parents. I do believe that God uses grandparents, aunts, uncles, and friends to help supplement when needs aren't met, but there is still a built-in need from the biological aspect. If a parent was physically present but emotionally shut down, there can still be a deficit in your heart and soul.

Unconditional Love

Our first and greatest need is to be loved, but not *just* loved—we need to be loved unconditionally, to know we have the love of both parents, regardless of our accomplishments or failures. The first way we receive God's love is through our parents. Many of us didn't receive unconditional love from our parents, which can make it difficult to trust that God's love is completely unconditional.

Many of our parents didn't receive unconditional love from their parents, so what they had to give may have been minimal because they may not have known how to fully love. They may have even given every drop of love they had, and yet your heart and soul still had a yearning for more.

I worked hard to get people to like me, to show me love. I have heard stories of, "I knew my parents loved me, and they were excellent providers, but I didn't really feel loved." Not feeling unconditional love is a depletion to our souls. If we feel unloved, the enemy can place lies in our hearts like, "I'm not loved. I'm not lovable." When we come into agreement with those lies, they will play out in our daily lives and relationships. Love is felt through the fulfilling of our emotional needs.

To Be Seen

To be seen and validated seeps into multiple emotional need categories. I believe the first piece of validation is the need to feel seen, knowing that you matter. To truly know you are seen fuels the feeling of being loved and being accepted. We see in Genesis 16:13 (NLT) when Hagar says, "You are the God who sees me," that she was immediately validated. The Lord asked where she come from (her past) and where she was going (future). I believe validating what happened before and what is happening in the present matters.

The first time I read that scripture, I could feel God giving me His validation and filling the areas where that was lacking. To be seen opens the heart to receive. For me, it enabled me to fully receive God's kindness.

When you feel seen by your parents as a child, it enables you to trust, to know that they support you, are in your corner, and that they deeply care. Validation makes us feel safe, heard, and cared for. When that validation isn't received, you can feel lonely, sad, discouraged and especially rejected as an adult.

Acceptance

Being loved unconditionally flows into the emotional need of acceptance. This is a fundamental emotional need that confirms belonging, to know that you have a place in family. It is crucial that you feel or felt like you belonged, that you were accepted. This need also helps confirm where we fit in God's family. If that need wasn't met, it leaves us feeling unsettled and lonely, sometimes like an outsider.

I was always searching for where I fit in, where I belonged, but feeling like I was so radically different from those around me, I just couldn't find my place. I believe a big part of this was my biological father being absent. Part of the truth of my identity was missing, and it left a hole in my heart. When we aren't secure in being accepted, the door to rejection is opened. Rejection is the opposite of acceptance. If we didn't feel like we belonged in our biological family, we can unintentionally expect rejection in our church family, friend groups, and community.

Affirmation

Affirmation is equally as important and is like acceptance—it gives us a sense of purpose and the pleasure and delight of our parents. It gives us worth and value, centers us as part of the family. When the need for affirmation is fulfilled, it will confirm that we fit or have a place in our natural family and helps us fit into God's family. When we aren't affirmed as children, we will begin working for that affirmation into adulthood. Many times, this results in becoming very performance driven, unable to stop and enjoy the work that's been done because you're trying to earn affirmation by pleasing people.

I was a workaholic with my career and a servaholic at church. I was restless but felt like I had to be a strong and independent woman. If I showed I needed others, I was afraid I would be or look weak. It was hard to step into my calling—or even to know exactly what that calling was. I took the lack of affirmation and decided that I didn't need anyone to affirm me. That self-sufficient posture in my heart was a red light that something was wrong.

One of my favorite examples of affirmation is in the Bible. We see that Jesus is affirmed by God the Father before He does even one miracle, sign, or wonder in His earthly ministry.

> After Jesus was baptized, He came up immediately out of the water; and behold, the heavens were opened, and he (John) saw the Spirit of God descending as a dove and lighting on Him (Jesus), and behold, a voice from heaven said, "This is My beloved Son, in whom I am well-pleased *and* delighted!"
> —Matthew 3:16-17 (AMP)

Quality Time

Another emotional need is quality time; it links us to our parents and family. In this quality time, it's also important to have fun, to have our parents engage in playtime. Unfortunately, there are many parents who have to make a choice—work to put food on the table or spend time helping with homework or playing a game. They had to make the hard choice to provide food. Even though the choice the parent made wasn't necessarily the wrong choice, it still had an impact. Or if a parent had an unhealthy balance with work and home life, it could have the same impact.

As adults, we can understand the decision our parent(s) had to make. In most situations as children, especially young children, that understanding may not have been there. This unmet need showed up a lot for me. I was always trying to get attention—being the best, the smartest, the funniest—yet my self-image was so poor. Our parents may have met our physical needs, with some giving out of the best they had to give, but still left us in great lack. The biggest way to meet this need is to enter your child's world instead of pulling them into yours. The quality time of, "I see you," "You matter," "What is happening in your day," etc. is significant in emotional growth.

Comfort

Comfort is another very real need, felt from the moment we are born. As children, there is a great need to be comforted by both our parents. To be soothed when hurting. To have someone come alongside us and bring comfort to our hearts and souls. When we fall, our parents wrap their arms around us and help us up. There is a time for correction and instruction, but the emotional need of comfort must have been met first. When that need isn't met, in our teenage years and into adulthood we learn how to self-comfort in unhealthy ways. Sometimes, you could be *very* needy, and this is where addictions can come in. If this need is unmet, we can become cold-hearted or closed off.

We read in the scriptures how important comfort is. So much so that Jesus promised that as He returned to the Father, He would leave us a comforter, the Holy Spirit.

> And I will ask the Father, and He will give you another Helper (Comforter, Advocate, Intercessor—Counselor, Strengthener, Standby), to be with you forever— the Spirit of Truth, whom the world cannot receive [and take to its heart] because it does not see Him or know Him, *but* you know Him because He (the Holy Spirit) remains with you *continually* and will be in you.
> —John 14:16-17 (AMP)

> As one whom his mother comforts, so I will comfort you;
> —Isaiah 66:13a (AMP)

Support

Having support as a child will help us engage in new things. When this need is met, our hearts will feel seen and loved, knowing that we have those in our corner to cheer us on and lift us up. This will affirm that we aren't alone and will aid in safety, giving our hearts hope and encouragement.

While growing up, I didn't feel like this need was met. As an adult, the fruit I displayed was being easily offended, and I would give up easily. If I couldn't be the best at something or be celebrated for my accomplishments, I wouldn't even try. Fear of failure gripped me. I started things but would be unable to complete them, even simple things like reading a book or working on a project.

The Bible says that hope deferred makes the heart sick. I believe that if you don't have adequate support, it brings on a spirit of discouragement. You can have a negative outlook on life, be unwilling to try new things, even feel hopelessness or a weariness toward living.

> Hope deferred makes the heart sick, But *when* the desire comes, *it is* a tree of life.
> —Proverbs 13:12 (NKJV)

Safety

Safety is another very important emotional need we have as children—to be able to trust the family and people around us. Safety equates stability and security, and it's where trust is built. When safety, trust, and security are broken, it leaves an open door to fear and to the enemy, and we don't get to pick which demon comes through. Often, the demon will come in and bring torment in our emotions, pulling us into fear, spiraling when something happens that we can't control.

Safety is so essential for a healthy heart, soul, and body. For me, not having my biological father in my home and the significant abuses I went through were the biggest culprits to this unmet need. Children need their biological father in their lives, both physically and emotionally. I believe in cases where the father is absent—either by choice, death, or even in cases of adoption—this creates a crack in our hearts where that need wasn't met. We will fill that crack or deficit with people and things that are unhealthy.

Maybe your story is different from mine and your father was physically there; it's important to consider if he was there emotionally. For me, this unmet need was compacted because I felt I could not trust my mom or Stepfather, which left me feeling like I had to fight for myself, I needed to protect myself, and I couldn't trust people. As a teenager and adult, I was able to mask my fear as being bold and assertive most of the time. People would say I had Type A personality, but now I realize there was a deep brokenness.

When my body got very sick and my immune system crashed, it was the year before the virus in 2019. When the pandemic occurred, I was crippled with fear, as were many other people in the world. The fear and insecurity of feeling like I couldn't trust others and that I physically wasn't safe (all the insecurity from my childhood) came rushing back in.

I was told that I needed to be physically safe because if I caught the virus, my lungs would not be able to fight it off and I could potentially die. Fear gripped me. The insecurity that I couldn't trust others came rushing to the surface. It was a hard season, especially since I had no idea of the depths of why I was so unsettled.

Story About the Unmet Emotional Need of Safety

I was in Texas, completing the classes to become an ordained minister. I had received the prophetic words, "God wants you to run," so I had started running again. I should have started with walking first, but I ran! I loved it, and when my feet hit the asphalt, I could feel the delight of God. It was exhilarating! I knew I wanted to continue running while we were out of town, so my husband helped me to map out a course.

Before one of my classes the next morning, as I was preparing to leave the hotel for the run, I realized I didn't have my pepper spray. A trembling panic filled me. My husband encouraged me that the route was safe, and we had marked it out. I had said I trusted God, but I was just trusting in myself. I ended up taking my husband's pocketknife and sticking it in my shorts, just in case I needed it.

Now, there is wisdom in protecting yourself, but I knew what I was feeling wasn't wisdom—something inside was off. I started my run and everything was fine. When a man drove by me and slowed down, the feeling inside made me want to vomit and fall to my knees, shaking. I was so unsettled. Not being protected as a little girl, not feeling safe, was resurfacing, even though it was about 40 years later. It was terrifying. The overreaction inside my body was a cue that what was happening in the moment was touching something that started way back in childhood.

The Fruit of Unmet Emotional Needs

There are no perfect parents—all parents make mistakes, even the best ones. Some were excellent providers of food and shelter but weren't able to fulfill the emotional needs we had. Many of them had no idea what emotional needs even were. We must position ourselves in Jesus with raw and honest prayers so Jesus can fill our hearts. That process will change our lives, giving us a new lens to see the world through, and will keep us from running to places that can't fulfill our hearts. Only He can fully supply all our needs, including emotional ones.

When we realize there was a deficit in our emotional needs, we then yield our hearts to Jesus to fill them. We see the need that wasn't met, and we pour out our heart in real and honest prayers. Jesus didn't die for us to live a life of just coping. He died for me to live an abundant life, to walk in healing and wholeness.

> I came that they may have *and* enjoy life, and have it in abundance [to the full, till it overflows].
> —John 10:10b (AMP)

When we slow down, truly listen to our hearts, and dive into what emotional needs are not being met, this awareness is where we meet God. Emotions have a voice, and they are speaking—it's just that, most of the time, we don't know what they're saying.

We must take the time to listen to our feelings, to listen to what is happening inside of us. Our feelings will tell a story, long after the pain is buried and forgotten. With the help of Holy Spirit and trusted people who walked this path before, there is full healing. God brought people into my life that were familiar with what I was experiencing to help my heart heal from the needs I had as a child that weren't met. This is the reason I'm sharing my story; my hope is it will help many get their hearts healed and live whole lives.

When I began to see a pattern, what some call fruit, I realized that loneliness can happen even in a room full of people. The need to be perfect or look perfect, the inability to truly trust God, being unable to leave things on the altar—all of this was the fruit of these unemotional needs.

I had an inability to rest, and I was exhausted. I worked too much to gain affirmation and acceptance. At church, I served too much and couldn't focus; I said yes to things I wanted to say no to out of fear of rejection. No matter how much I slept, I was tired . . . my soul was tired.

I read book after book about the rest of God, implemented spiritual disciplines, and incorporated Sabbath, but I just couldn't get my body, mind, or soul to fully rest. There was no settling inside of my heart. I was easily offended, critical, and quick to be defensive. If I was in control of my life and the lives of my family, everything was fine, but if something happened—a sickness, accident, etc.—and I didn't have control, fear gripped me.

Not being comforted led to my seeking comfort in things not of God, like shopping on impulse and too much scrolling, believing I had to provide my worth. All the behavior an attempt to get the unmet needs from childhood met in adult adulthood. When we become adults, the needs don't stop. They are still there, and if we haven't processed them not being met in childhood, they will be magnified in adulthood.

I had thought that my actions were just sin and I needed to act better, but the behavior was from those unmet emotional needs from childhood. If you read my symptoms, or fruit and see those in your life, be encouraged. Do any of these strike a chord with you:

- Working to feel loved, fighting feelings of loneliness, sadness, discouragement, and especially rejection.

- Unsettled or lonely, like an outsider. Feeling like you're searching for where you fit in, where you belong, but thinking you're so different from those around you.

- Restless and feeling like you must be strong and independent.

- Hard to step into your calling or know exactly what that calling is.

- Performance driven, unable to stop and enjoy the work that's been done.

- Being a people pleaser, fixer.

- Being very needy and possibly fighting additions, obsessive compulsive disorder, anxiety, or feelings of defeat.

- Being fearful, having unexplained illnesses.

- Giving up easily and being unable to complete projects, etc.

- Easily discouraged, negative outlook on life, and being unwilling to try new things. Feeling hopelessness, sometimes even a weariness toward living, or overthinking.

- Unable to trust God, unable to relax and be at ease.

- Unable to trust and get close to others.

We can't go backwards on our own, but we can with the Lord. We can forgive and release those we held responsible for our unmet needs, repent for seeking to have our needs met outside of God, and then we can begin to heal. Healing enables us to hold our cup up to the Father to let Him fill it, giving us affirmation and acceptance as He gives us safety and stability. Those around us add to our cups, but they don't fill them. Only God can truly fill the cup to overflowing.

More than the negative fruit from needs not being met are the lies that the enemy gives. When we agree with lies from the enemy, we give him a legal right in our heart.

Just a few of the lies I believed were:

- I'm not worthy of being loved.
- No one really cares about me.
- No one really sees me.
- I don't fit in; I don't belong.
- I'm a burden to other people.
- My needs aren't important.
- I must fight for myself.
- No one will protect me.

When these needs aren't met, there will be an inability to express what we need and what we feel. It's hard to bond with other people, especially emotionally. There's usually much fear and lack of trust. Rejection will seep in, especially if the need of attention was not meant.

When we believe lies, we can pray through them by repenting for believing the lie over the truth and then coming out of agreement with the lie. I encourage you not to go through the lies all together, but each one individually.

PROMPT:

I want to encourage you to dig into any unmet emotional needs. If unmet in childhood, they were automatically a deficit in adulthood because we still have those needs. But if you let the Lord heal the deficit, Jesus can then fill your cup so those around you can add their splashes, and you'll overflow into their lives so they're able to feel the love of God.

From the unmet emotional needs that were mentioned, here are more symptoms I was seeing:

- Feeling drained from ministering, even just listening, to others
- Insecurity
- Inability to rest
- Easily offended and critical
- Lack of boundaries with work and church
- Being a workaholic and servaholic (at church)
- Quick to say yes, even when my heart was saying no

- Feelings of rejection
- Perfectionism
- Inability to trust people
- Feeling like I had to fix and take care of those around me
- Controlling
- Inability to be comforted, settled
- Overspending
- Too much social media

I wrote letters for each unmet emotional need to my mom, dad, and stepfather, though they were not written with the intention of being sent—they were for me only. I explained in detail about the pain felt, the deficit that was there, and how it had affected my life. I wrote several of the letters multiple times until I felt the pain release.

I forgave them again since the pain was no longer buried, and journaled my heart to Jesus in real, honest, and raw prayers, about what I was feeling and how overwhelmed my heart was. I grieved the significant loss I felt both as a little girl and an adult.

Then I gave Jesus space to speak back to my heart to soothe me. I wrote down His words that washed my heart, bringing comfort and peace.

I worked through the lies I had believed, renounced them, came out of agreement with them, and replaced them with the truth of what the scriptures said. I declared God's words over my heart daily.

And then I just sat with Jesus, letting Him wash away the pain, hurt, and disappointment from my heart and soul.

It was not easy, but the fruit of peace was undeniable.

Chapter Sixteen

Rejection

Where there's favoritism there will be rejection.

When there are unmet emotional needs, they can compound the strong feelings of rejection and possibly lead us into expecting to be rejected, even if the person in our current life is safe.

I shared testimony earlier of journaling God's voice and how God told me He would bring my father straight to me. God was faithful and did exactly that. It was and is a miraculous story, and I'm still in awe of God's goodness and faithfulness!

I want to share a second part about what happened. When my mom told me her story how she met my dad and their relationship, she also told me about when she found out she was pregnant. She went to the restaurant where he worked and told him, and she detailed their conversation to me.

When I found my dad, before I even asked, he told me that he couldn't recall any intimate details of their relationship, that they were just friends and never "slept" together. Eventually, he admitted to a relationship with my mom, but said that he never knew about me (even though my mom shared details about when she told him). I was so desperate for unconditional love, acceptance, and affirmation, that even at 38 years old, I just dismissed every red flag. His wife assured me that he had forgotten thing because he'd had a serious stoke years prior. It didn't feel right with me, but I dismissed the whole thing without processing, just blindly trusting.

Around the time of my birthday, my husband and I were living in the house we had purchased in the town where my Dad lived, and we invited my dad and his wife over for dinner to celebrate. After dinner, we were relaxing in the living room, and my dad began talking. He talked and he talked . . . and then he started talking about my mom.

The atmosphere shifted, and I leaned in to listen closer. The language barrier made it difficult to have deeper conversations with him, so whenever he would spoke, I listened intently. He began to share with me, almost verbatim, the story my mom told surrounding when she told him that she was pregnant.

Up until this point, he told me that he never knew about the pregnancy. But suddenly he was going on about how, on a Wednesday at 2:00 p.m., she came by the restaurant and told him she was pregnant. She then confirmed to him that the baby was his because she had not been with anyone else.

As my dad sat freely sharing these details, my insides shook. The rejection and deep pain I felt was from all the way back in the womb.

The enemy began feeding me lies like, "Had your dad been there, the men wouldn't have hurt you. The abuse is his fault." Lies like these will feel like truth because they came from pain that was felt in your core, and it seemed like they were suffocating me. I took all of what I felt and the lies circling my heart back to the secret place, where my God time is.

This pain took some time to get through, and I knew that more forgiveness was needed. I believe forgiveness comes in layers. What you are forgiving for in this season could be different from the last season. I needed to forgive my dad for not looking for me, though he knew where my family lived. When I was at my nana's, I was only about 10-15 minutes from his house. The pain of this rejection hit so deep. I had to forgive him for not taking responsibly as my father and protector.

Then a step further, I needed to repent for the judgment I immediately made against him: "How could you? You were the one who said you were a Christian. How could you just abandon me? How could you lie to me?"

Remember that these kinds of judgments are statements made from pain regarding the person you hold responsible for hurting you. When the statements are made from pain, the sin can't be judged—only the person. When you judge the person, you apply an identity to them, but only the Lord can judge fairly and righteously. That is why it is so important to forgive and release.

Recognize the judgment, repent for it, and release it to God. Go a step further and pray, "God, I release this judgment to you. Today, I repent for making it, God, I put this judgment to death on the cross, and I ask you to resurrect new life in my heart." The resurrection power of Jesus will reside in the place where the judgment once rested so it can no longer hold the pain there.

The new trust I had fully given was crushed, all without him even realizing it. Out of my zeal and excitement, I fully trusted, but now I realize trust is built over time. I have been loving from the abundance of emotion and not the fullness of God. There would be another similar incident to come, more painful than this one, but I was gaining tools to process. For example, the strategy heaven was releasing to fight the enemy's power in my heart and life. And as I was growing, I was learning boundaries.

When pain happens—and it will happen because no one is immune to it—we must stop and pause long enough to gain our voice and put words to what we're feeling. We then need to sit with Jesus and go deep into that place to let Him touch it. Only then can the pain be healed and removed. He touches the places neglected in childhood with His balm that brings healing. I sat in the arms of Jesus, my tears landing on God's chest, where He caught them. I poured out my heart and described the immense rejection I was feeling. My life changed again that day; the rejection I felt was so big, but God was bigger!

It seemed like people don't like to talk about the hard parts, only the glorious and happy parts. However, the hard parts are where the love, acceptance, security, affirmation, and the belonging to Jesus became real. I sat with Him, pouring out all the pain I felt. Through the healing of Jesus, I was able to reposition myself as my Heavenly father's daughter and receive the love He has to offer me, feeling His delight fill my emotional deficits. In the space where I felt like an orphan, I became a daughter.

Then, as my cup was overflowing from God's love, I was able to fully receive the measure of love from my biological father that he had to give. He couldn't fully fill my cup, because his cup wasn't full from his own parents. God had given me revelation that I belong to Him; it went from head knowledge to heart revelation, and that changes everything.

> For it was always in His (God the Father) perfect plan to adopt us as his delightful children, through our union with Jesus, the Anointed One, so that his tremendous love that cascades over us would glorify his grace—for the same love he has for the Beloved, Jesus, he has for us. And this unfolding plan brings Him great pleasure!
> —Ephesians 1:5-6 (TPT)

When I sat with Jesus, positioning myself as His daughter with very honest and raw prayers, He pulled me close to His heart and whispered to me that He understood. He had been rejected, too, by those He loved. He brought comfort to my aching heart and peace, wiping my tears and mending my heart. Jesus spoke softly and reminded me that I was seen by Him, that His love truly was and is unconditional because He is the only perfect One. His love filled my thirsty soul. The desert inside my chest turned into an oasis, where Jesus came, touched, filled, and released His full measure of love into me. I'll never be the same.

As I processed the rejection I felt, first from my mother and stepfather and then from my biological father, I was able to heal. I have been able to see how I was rejecting people in the current day. I realized that if I was going to step into my calling and purpose, that, much like Joseph in the Bible, my heart would have to heal. I needed to make hard choices to forgive and release, and I would need to repent for the judgments I made, surrendering my heart fully to the Lord to be received by Him.

I was living in the lies instead of the truth. The truth would set me free, but for that to happen, it meant I was bound by the lies.

I began to understand that, in Christ, I wouldn't be forsaken, that though my father mother forsook me, He never would. I recognized the promises of God, and because I had processed through the pain, the promises of God had space in my heart to take root.

I want to encourage you to dig deep. Ask Holy Spirit to reveal who rejected you and who you need to forgive and release.

The Lord spoke to me recently and said that though we hold onto the thorns that hurt deeply, He wants to give us roses that are thornless. There's an exchange that God has for us, but we must make the choice to say yes to healing.

No more coping, only healing.

Chapter Seventeen

Lies

If the soil in our hearts has lies planted, the truth cannot take root.

Lies are tricky—they come in the form of thoughts bathed in feelings that make them seem true. They come especially when our hearts are hurt, when painful things have happened, like disappointment or the loss of something precious. The feelings and thoughts are so real, many times familiar to what we have heard and felt before, it's easy to fail prey to them, especially when there are wounds remaining in our hearts and souls. They are an attack on our identity and calling.

We read in 2 Corinthians 2:11 (AMP) that we are not ignorant of Satan's schemes: "to keep Satan from taking advantage of us; for we are not ignorant of his schemes."

The verse starts out with "to keep Satan from taking advantage of us." If there are lies in our heart, the enemy has access to take advantage of us—many times without us even realizing it. When we look at the original meaning of the word "schemes" in Greek, the word is *noema,* which means "thoughts." The verse can then be read: "to keep Satan from taking advantage of us; for we are not ignorant of Satan's thoughts," including his lies.

When thoughts come into our minds, we must take them captive to find the source. Are the thoughts mine, God's, or Satan's? Whose thoughts they are is very important. When thoughts are placed in our mind and we receive them, even if we don't realize it, the agreement with a lie allows it to have a spiritual authority in our lives.

Maybe the lie is something that seems as innocent as trying on a new dress; You see yourself in the mirror and the thought comes, "I look so fat and ugly." When you agree with that thought, that lie, it then has permission to take root. That agreement has opened the door for the enemy to assault you with more lies, producing fruit. One of the biggest for me was insecurity. If that lie resides long enough, a spirit of self-hatred can have access. How can you love others if you hate yourself? The Bible says we are to love our neighbors as we love ourselves.

If you agree with a lie, "Yes, I do look fat and ugly," you open the door to darkness and the enemy. Remember, you don't get to pick which demon comes through. The outcome, a direct attack at you, the creation of God and made in His image, now believes a simple lie with deep roots. This example may seem trivial, but that's how sin starts—small. Over time, it grows, and the next lie the enemy tempts you with will have even deeper roots. A door to self-hatred has now been opened.

Lies are always an attack on our calling and our identity. They will stunt or stop both if given access by your belief in them, which is your agreement.

Lies are like weeds—they consume the good nutrients in the soil of your heart, yet produce only negative or bad fruit. That fruit manifests in more thoughts and impacts every facet of our lives and relationships. Lies must be dug up and replaced with truth. Jesus said the truth will set us free.

> And you will know the truth, and the truth will set you free.
> —John 8:32 (NLT)

To be set free, you must first have been bound. That's what lies do. They bind you to the kingdom of darkness, wrapping around you like chains. They open the door to the enemy and consume space that was set apart for only goodness and truth to be planted, to occupy. Sometimes lies will contain partial truth to be even more convincing, but what they produce will reveal the motive of what was planted.

I had been taught in church that God was all you need—a piece of truth that was twisted, planting a big lie in my heart. Many times, when I should have been receiving from the people God had set around me, I stepped outside of it, thinking that I just needed more God time or to worship more, maybe learn more scriptures. I thought that because God was all I needed, then the fact that I was still in need must have meant something was wrong with me. It is true that we need God's principles, ways, love, compassion, and mercy—the list goes on and on—but that's not all.

We also need safe people and community. For example, if you believe the lie, "I can't trust people because they will hurt me," you will keep the bad out . . . but you will also keep the good out. The freedom I began feeling when I realized we need God *and more* was unlike anything I had experienced before. I threw out traditional man-made theology and started searching the scriptures with a new lens. What I saw was the beauty of Jesus and how His life on earth is one for us to follow.

He showed us the importance of community; this is where we are healed. Isolation is a tactic of the enemy. We have a real enemy who constantly whispers thoughts that are tempting for us to agree with. When Jesus walked upon the earth, He had a close circle of friends in Peter, James, and John. Then came the disciples, then the 70. If Jesus needed companions, so do we.

I bought the lie that God was all I needed, and soon that lie had invaded all parts of my mind. I began taking on shame, believing that I wasn't good enough or strong enough. The one lie planted in the soil of my heart yielded a terrible crop, one that would need to be torn down and replaced with good seeds. The plan of God for my life and your life is one that is truly good and that you will prosper in! One where the truth has set us free.

> "For I know the plans I have for you," says the Lord. "They are plans for good and not for disaster, to give you a future and a hope.
> —Jeremiah 29:11 (NLT)

God began teaching me that He wasn't like earthly fathers or the men who had hurt me. He would not harm me nor abandon me. He was teaching me truth.

I didn't realize I was believing lies that stemmed from the absence of my biological father and from the abuse of my stepfather. I would need to step through the door that God was calling me to by repenting for believing a lie and coming out of agreement with the lies, one by one.

What we go through as children will affect us in adulthood if it's not healed. I remember being taught that because God is all powerful, everything comes from Him. That even sickness came from God because He was teaching a lesson, or wanted His glory to be shown, or even that sickness could come upon you because you didn't obey God so just be thankful it's not worse. I had a very distorted view of God. As I began stripping off the lies that held me like chains, I could finally breathe again; I was able to then begin receiving the Truth. The voice of God will break the power of lies.

When I was sick, I prayed and prayed until it felt like all my faith was gone. I wanted to be better; some days, it would take everything in me just to get out of bed. One day, Jesus spoke to me, "Beloved, I am not using sickness to teach you a lesson, but I am moving in closer and holding your hand through this. I won't leave your side."

Those tender yet powerful words of truth gave me the strength to renounce the lie that sickness was upon me to "teach me a lesson." I prayed a simple prayer like, "I renounce and come out of agreement with the lie that God is teaching me a lesson by putting sickness upon me, and I declare the truth that Jesus is with me. He is holding my hand, and He won't leave my side." The tender voice of God would give me strength to fight the lies. And whenever the enemy tried to give me that lie again, I stopped it. I had heard the voice of Truth, and that's who I was partnering with.

I've come to realize that when there is pain, wounding, and disappointment, there are always lies that are planted or given. In my life, it felt like lies had weights on them that held my heart down and blocked hope. Many times, lies come with very strong emotion and foul language—I don't mean like profanity, but words that curse. They usually condemn or blame others, yourself, or God. They question if God is good, if He's even real or cares. They typically have words like never or always.

The biggest shadow I've seen with lies is shame. *Lies carry shame.* When our souls ache, the enemy will slide in with a lie that sounds so much like truth that we accept it, giving the enemy access to our souls. We need to process the pain and give words to what happened, to forgive and release the pain, possibly process the memory, or repent for judgments, and we need to ask Holy Spirit what lies we are believing. We repent for believing those lies and come out of agreement with them to uproot them from our heart. We replace the lie with truth, and then Jesus brings good fruit, even orchards.

Testimony

At a women's event, I had shared my testimony and about the seriousness of lies. There was an older woman there, and I could tell she had a long history with Jesus. She shared with me that a piece of my testimony had truly ministered to her heart and that she had a very similar event happen in her family. I had asked her if I could pray over her, to which she was very open. I then heard God say, "Ask her what lies she is believing." When I spoke that aloud to her, she instantly grew defensive and told me she wasn't believing any lies, that she has a very close relationship with Jesus. I just listened to her.

Then Holy Spirit whispered to me the exact lie she was believing. I looked in her eyes and spoke very gently to her the truth that God had given me. It was the exact opposite of the lie. As I spoke out the truth, she began weeping and collapsed in my arms. I could feel heaven over her. Jesus, who is the Truth, crushed the lie of the enemy that she had been believing. Instantly, she was set free from the condemning shame from believing it was her fault the incident happened. She came out of agreement with that lie and replaced it with the truth. The truth was declared, and she was set free for the peace of God to settle over her heart. It was beautiful.

I have ministered to countless people, and when I asked them, "Are there any lies you are believing?" they almost always assure me that there are none. The problem with being deceived is *you're deceived*. Lies hide in pain, usually condemning you and giving you a cloak of shame to wear.

When Holy Spirit began reteaching me this concept, I truly didn't think I was believing any lies, but I know His voice, and I was open to Him. So I gave Him my yes, and He began gently showing me lies that I had believed about myself and others. Lies like, "They'll never change—that's just how they are," seemed small, but they carried powerful consequences with them. I began to understand the root of many poor choices stemming from lies believed about ourselves and of others. Lies from painful situations.

Possible lies about yourself:

My life will never change. My family will never change.
I am not enough.
I am not smart enough. I don't have enough education.
I am not important. No one sees me.
I don't have a voice. What I have to say doesn't matter.
I am replaceable. I am not valuable.
I am a burden. I am too much.
I am broken and cannot be fixed. I am beyond help.
I am unlovable. No one truly loves me.
No one understands me. It's better to be alone.

I'm inadequate. I don't belong.
It's up to me to do it all.
I must fight for myself.

Possible lies about God:

God is not good.
God is distant and doesn't care.
God has abandoned me.
God doesn't see me. He doesn't protect His people.
God is teaching me a lesson, punishing me.
God cannot protect me. He isn't safe.
God is weak and powerless in my situation.
God's love isn't for me; it's conditional.
God is angry at me. God is disappointed in me.
God is not trustworthy.
God is setting me up to fail. He has not prepared me.
God demands perfection.

I want to encourage you that when you're in your God time, ask Holy Spirit what lies you're believing. Or if any of those ones I listed above stand out to you, I want to encourage you in this simple prayer.

*Jesus, I have believed the lie **[state the lie]**, and I repent for that now. I renounce the lie **[repeat the lie]**, and I come out of agreement with this lie. I declare the truth **[state the truth - this is usually the exact opposite of the lie]** in Jesus' name.*

Truths:

God is good.
God is close to my heart and cares deeply for me.
God will not abandon me.
God sees me, and He protects His children.
God isn't punishing me.
God will protect me; He is safe.
God is all powerful in my situation.
God's love for me isn't conditional but endless.
God is not angry at me. God is not disappointed in me.
God is trustworthy.
God is setting me up for success and has prepared me for all I face.
God doesn't demand perfection but is pleased with me.
God can be trusted.

Take a piece of paper and draw a line down the center of it. On the left side, make a list of lies that you believed about yourself, God, or others. On the right side, across from each lie, write out the truth (which is exactly the opposite of the lie). Search the scriptures to find the word of God that counteracts the lie you believed. Put that truth on sticky notes or on index cards, then place them on your mirrors, the refrigerator, in your car—wherever you will see them often. And declare the truth over your heart; it will take root, and it will bring forth an orchard of good fruit.

Chapter Eighteen

Grieving

Pain must be felt to be released.

WHAT I HAVE EXPERIENCED is that when most people hear the word "grieving," it is quickly met with, "Oh, I'm not grieving, I'm fine." People often believe grief is just the emotion of sadness, but it encompasses many emotions, such as shock, anger, sadness, despair, and so on. Grief is also perceived to only be felt when a loved one has passed away, but it's so much more. We are called to grieve anything that has been lost that deeply affected our hearts. When we take time to grieve, we take time to embrace the sorrow and loss we experienced.

I have grieved the loss of my maternal grandmother, my nana, who held the place of a mom in my heart. I grieved the loss of innocence from my childhood and the loss of growing up without a father. I have grieved the expectations of what I thought certain relationships would look like. And I grieved the loss of relationship with those who are close to my heart, though they remain alive.

We grieve anything that causes our hearts sadness. We must process this feeling because grief deeply affects our hearts. It can linger through our souls in such a way that it leaves residue in every season and every relationship of our lives.

Grieving is hard, very hard. But when we face our grief, we no longer deny the pain we feel and acknowledge what was lost. In that acknowledgment and those strong emotions, welcoming God into the process, healing can begin to take place in our hearts.

I have ministered to those who have grieved less than me, and I have ministered to those who have grieved in a much greater capacity than I can even understand. All grief needs to be felt and processed to heal. We can't skip through the hard stuff; press on, keep going, and expect your heart to fully heal. We must pause and process what was lost so that we can gain what God has for us. When we process, we can then set our gaze forward and take the next step.

Loss of my grandmother

I shared earlier in this book about how fond my heart was of my nana. She was my rock, a constant, the one who I felt love from, my safe place. Nana was getting older—about 89 years old—but was still spunky, and she had such kind eyes. Every Saturday, my daughter and I would go to her home, pick her up, take her out for breakfast, and then get some groceries and enjoy ice cream sundaes. We would end the day with fresh sheets on her bed, a bath (complete with lotion and lots of baby powder), a pedicure, and freshly polished nails. This was our routine for years.

One July, around my birthday, I noticed her health was different. She had been placed on oxygen and didn't feel the best. Though her health was declining, I didn't expect her to pass away anytime soon. I suppose you're never ready for someone so dear to your heart to pass away.

I was traveling for work and was in a different state at the time. I had talked to my aunt that morning through her soft sobs as she said, "Mama just doesn't sound good." I remember saying something like, "It's going to be okay," never expecting what would happen next.

I was in a meeting with a few of my coworkers, and we were sitting around a huge U-shaped table along with several folks from what would be my new account. And then God spoke to me. He said, "She's with Me now."

His words took my breath away. I thought, "I rebuke you Satan—surely that's not God."

I then watched my sales rep answer his phone and walk out of the room. When he returned, he came straight to me and said, "Can I speak to you for a moment?"

My insides trembled. I stepped out of the room, looked him in the eyes, and said, "Don't you dare say it to me."

He replied, in a soft voice, "You need to call your husband."

I told him that I would sit back down in the meeting and pretend he didn't just say that to me. As I sat down and the reality of what God had spoken began to take root, I leaned over to a different coworker and said, "Find me a flight home."

The people God had surrounded me with at my job had become like family to me. Two special women at the company I worked for were already in contact with my husband and were getting me a flight home.

I called my husband, and when he said hello, I immediately knew it was true. My nana not only adored me, but she loved him deeply, and he was hurting too—not just for himself, but for me and our daughter. The two special women who were working to get me a flight home were already at our home, arms wrapped around my daughter, both certainly a gift from God to my family.

After our meeting, my main sales rep, who had told me to call my husband, drove me to the hotel. I was in the van, my head between my knees, in gut-wrenching sobs. *How could she be gone? How could God take her without me by her side? Is this real? Is this really happening?*

I got to the airport, and my sales rep took care of everything. He showed his cell phone to the airline representative—I'm sure it must've said something about what I was going through. Airport workers ushered me from place to place to ensure I caught the correct flight.

At the time of Nana's passing, there was a particular type of bracelet that was very popular called silly band bracelets. They were basically rubber bands that came in different colors and, when not on your wrist, would be a variety of shapes, including objects, animals, etc. When I boarded the plane and sat in my seat, I looked at my feet, and I saw a white silly band in the shape of a crown. And God spoke to me, "Today, she laid her crown at My feet."

I picked up the silly band as tears flooded my face. I couldn't hold them back. In the process of Nana passing and my having no immediate family around me, God reminded me that He was with me and would not forsake me, my pain, or my desperation.

I arrived home that night, and my husband, daughter, and I went straight to my mom's. A very dear friend had already sent food to ensure we were taken care of, which was truly a blessing because the next day was hard, to say the least. There were a lot of people coming and going, and I was so angry—I was in shock that she was gone, and sadness engulfed me like angry waves. My daughter, sister, aunt, and I went next door to my nana's house and sat on her porch, something we did together frequently.

Nana loved hummingbirds, but it had probably been about five years since we had seen any at her home. I sat on her porch, filled with anger. God's presence seemed to have vanished overnight. I whispered to Him, "God, You are a liar. You said that You would never leave me, yet, in my deepest need, You cannot be found."

Tears streamed down my face, and just as my thought finished, this hummingbird flew right up to my face, its beak almost touching the bridge between my eyes, and God spoke, "I will never leave you, nor forsake you." I learned in that moment that my outrageous—some would say foolish—prayers didn't push God away, but He came in closer. It would be years later, maybe a decade, that God would speak to me, and say, "Your pain is a sweet aroma to me, as My son died to heal it." Our strong emotion and extreme prayers do not push God away, and neither do our questions. Instead, He leans in closer, paying careful attention to the cries of His child.

When my nana passed, I didn't have a recipe for grieving. I just called on Jesus over and over, and He sent safe people to love me and take me by the hand. It was a long journey. I remember thinking, "It's been over a year—shouldn't I be able to get through one day without crying?" but everyone's timeline is different.

When someone you love passes away, or as you process through loss in life, try walking through the below steps. Whether that loss is friendship, a career, marriage, the loss of childhood, grieving through things just didn't go as you thought they would, or loss because you expected life would be different now. All losses are important and must be grieved. When we don't process through the things we lose, they pile up. And then when we experience a new loss, what is felt will be compounded by previous losses that we weren't grieved.

Remember, when we don't grieve, the pain will come out in some manner. Sometimes by depression, anxiety, hopelessness, despair, bitterness, addiction (to substance, food, or people), sickness, and more. If we don't process grief as it happens—as well as going back to process what we have lost in the past—then even small losses in our current world will seem massive and overwhelming.

Grieving Steps

1. Shock, Anger, and Sadness

In 2010 when my nana passed, the first emotion I felt was shock. As God whispered to me that she was with Him, the shock seemed to pulsate through my body and my mind could not make sense of it.

I became angry for God allowing it, the remorse and sadness for not being there. Sorrow would wash over me like a strong tide in the ocean, many times taking the very breath from my lungs and drowning me.

When I began looking at what I lost in my childhood, the shock, anger, and sadness was overwhelming. I saw how the losses from my childhood were impacting my current situations, but because I was acknowledging the losses, I was able to embrace the strong emotions and begin a grieving journey.

We must take the time to feel and acknowledge what we have lost. The person, the life, the relationship, the expectation of what we thought life would be. To embrace the shock, the anger, and the sadness. To feel the effect and magnitude of the loss. But we cannot remain in this place. I wrote out all my anger in letters to the person I held responsible for the loss. Some of the anger was held against those who hurt me, and some was against God. My strong emotions didn't push God away, but pulled Him closer.

Many times, we get stuck in the shock, anger, and sadness, and we circle around in those emotions. We must press into the next step.

I looked up what "shock" meant—to feel like the breath has been knocked out of you, to be shaken up, to be struck with fear, unnerved, confused. So much of this resonated with my heart and my soul. So, I wrote out what was happening in my heart, telling the Lord the shock I was feeling, having no idea of what was lost or buried.

I also read up on what anger looked like. At first, I didn't realize how angry I was, but then I started reading descriptions like frustration, being distant or withdrawn, being easily irritated, skeptical, resentful, even devastated. Again, my heart could relate and seemed to feel every one of these emotions at once.

I then looked up sadness. It could look like being lonely, easily bored, or feeling powerless, abandoned, or remorseful. And again, it felt like the definition of these words were describing what was happening in my heart.

In my journal, I wrote out to the Lord what was happening and how I was feeling. At the end, I wrote, "Lord, I release this to You."

2. Face what was lost

I had to face what happened and accept that I had experienced a significant loss. A funeral had to be planned; I couldn't pretend that nothing had happened or that life was going to remain the same. I would need to embrace the fact that life was going to be different. We would no longer spend Saturdays with Nana having breakfast, grocery shopping, and doing pedicures together. I had lost something so precious. More than time, I felt like I lost unconditional love and support. I lost comfort.

As I begin grieving losses from childhood, I had to acknowledge that, while finding my father at age 38 was a miraculous experience, I still needed him when I was a little girl. Not having him was a significant loss.

I also had to face the loss of relationships that were significant to my heart that would never be the same. There was loss of trust, and the reality of what happened felt like it was shaking me to my core.

I journaled, writing out what happened, the reality of all I lost. I faced how my life was different and what the loss meant to me, and how it affected me and those I love.

3. Forgiveness

I started asking myself, "Who do I blame? Who do I hold responsible?" As I answered those questions, I began releasing forgiveness. I walked through forgiving God, not because He had done anything wrong, but because I held Him responsible for allowing my nana's passing at a time when I couldn't be by her side. I forgave myself for being away on business, though I couldn't have known.

I forgave my mom for allowing things to happen, my dad for walking away, the men for hurting me, and myself for the poor decisions I had made. The more forgiveness I chose to release, the more the pain left my heart.

I began writing letters of "I forgive you for . . . and it made me feel . . ." This helped pull out the emotions that needed to be felt and released. When you write out how something made you feel, it can help you identify what lies you could possibly be believing because of the pain and loss.

4. Giving voice to what happened

I realized that the pain inside me must gain a voice and be heard in safe places. As I began to share my heart and what I was feeling, the heaviness lifted from me. As I verbally acknowledged my experiences and what I had lost, it was as if I was allowing God to comfort me using the arms of those who cared for me. I didn't shy away from sharing that my heart was broken but I gave voice to my pain.

I had passed through the shock, anger, and sadness and moved into recognizing what I've lost and forgiving. Once that occurred, sharing and grieving my loss allowed me to receive comfort from God and others. It allowed me to feel without feeling like I was drowning.

5. *Truth and Lies*

I had to come out of agreement with lies that I had believed, like lies around Nana's death, such as my being there could've made a difference, that I could have loved her better, or I could've spent more time with her. Some of the lies seem to have veins of truth in them, yet were covered in a residue that was not truth. What they produced was not light, but darkness.

In many of my losses, I had believed the lies that what had happened to me was my fault. Lies such as, "Had I not been at that place at that time, such a terrible incident wouldn't have happened."

As I went through each loss, whether a death or a loss in childhood or throughout my life, I would ask Holy Spirit, "What lies am I believing?" As He shone light on those lies, I would renounce them by coming out of agreement with them and then speaking out the truth in place of them, uprooting the lies from my heart and planting truth in the soil.

God's word is truth. I embraced scriptures, the Bible, and the truth. I spent time in the book of Psalms and found comfort in the words penned by the psalmist David. He wrote bold and real prayers. The words brought comfort and echoed the truth that God was listening to my cries, that He was close to the brokenhearted and those crushed and spirit. I was both.

I wrote out truth statements from the lies I had believed by using the opposite of what I felt. An example would be: when I felt unworthy, the truth was that I was worthy of being loved, protected, cared for, and cared about.

6. Acceptance and Receiving God's Peace

I had to acknowledge that my nana was gone and I couldn't change that. Life was different. I had to face the fact that she would miss many milestones in my life, that I wouldn't be able to hear her voice or see her smile again in this life. I was going to have to walk through some painful days and establish new routines, but I wouldn't do this alone—God was with me, and I could receive this truth.

As I grieved the loss of my innocence in childhood, I acknowledged that what happened to me couldn't be undone. I couldn't gain back my childhood, what was taken, or the security that was lost. I had to acknowledge that it really did happen and that it affected me deeply. My childhood was different, shadowed in much pain, dysfunction, and hurt. I had to face what happened and no longer sugarcoat it into something that didn't exist or make excuses for the ones who caused the pain.

What I finally *knew* was that God was with me, and His peace was transcending through what had been lost, bringing me into a place of peace. I wrote out this step to the Lord, and He gave me an exchange of sadness and mourning for joy. A beautiful exchange. The Bible calls it beauty for ashes.

Peace was the evidence that had I passed through the valley of grieving. In the psalms, David called it the valley of the shadow of death. I had walked through this valley, sometimes very slowly, where it felt like I was only crawling. The demanding sadness and reality of what has been lost was being replaced with the presence of God and His peace. The heaviness was replaced with light, the ashes with beauty.

> . . . he will give a crown of beauty for ashes, a joyous blessing instead of mourning, festive praise instead of despair.
>
> —Isaiah 61:3 (NLT)

> Now let your unfailing love comfort me, just as you promised me, your servant.
>
> —Psalms 119:76 (NLT)

Yea, though I walk through the valley of the shadow of death, I will fear no evil; For You *are* with me; Your rod and Your staff, they comfort me.

—Psalms 23:4 (NKJV)

Even when their paths wind through the dark valley of tears, they dig deep to find a pleasant pool where others find only pain. He gives to them a brook of blessing filled from the rain of an outpouring.

—Psalms 84:6 (TPT)

Encouragement:

God sees you; He sees you and your pain and your tears. He also sees you when you resist and are in denial—He loves you in both. We all experience loss in this life, but if we do not process losses, they will stockpile, and the effect and feeling of them will be much greater and our capacity much lighter. I was 44 years old when I grieved losing my grandfather, though I was around nine years old when he passed away. As a 40+ woman, I realized that when he passed, my feeling of security was lost. As I grieved losing security as a little girl, I dug deeper in that and realized that I had never fully grieved losing my Pawpaw. I mourned, I wept, I renounced lies that my security was only in him, and I declared the truth of where security is really found. I walked through grieving, and I came off of the path with joy.

Part of grieving is pressing in. Don't stop. As you are in one stage, keep pressing into the next stage. Everyone's timeline is different, but the point is that you continue walking. David said in Psalms 23, "**I walk through** the valley of the shadow . . ." Don't camp out, but keep walking through.

As you look back over your life, ask Holy Spirit what you need to grieve, what you need to process. He is faithful to lead us on the path of righteousness, no longer a visitation of peace, but a habitation.

> And the effect of righteousness will be peace [internal and external], and the result of righteousness will be quietness and confidence and trust forever. My people shall dwell in a peaceable habitation, in safe dwellings, and in quiet resting-places.
> —Isaiah 32:17-18 (AMPC)

Dear one, peace is your portion.

Chapter Nineteen
Keep going

> Even when your path takes me through the valley of deepest darkness, fear will never conquer me, for you already have!
>
> —Psalms 23:4a (TPT)

Our pain is a sweet aroma to the Lord, as it calls out to Him for His touch. We don't have a lot of sacrifices we can give God, but our pain and our praise are two sacrifices we can lift to Him. We are not called to keep or nurture pain, but it is our responsibly to come to God and say, "Jesus, I welcome You into my pain." It is in our weakness that He is strong. Our weakness and neediness draw the compassion of Jesus as we also welcome Him into that place. Weakness and neediness aren't our shame but our gift that we surrender to Jesus.

In the journey of life, we must keep going, putting one foot in front of the other. In the journey of healing, we do this by searching our hearts, bringing any pain we feel to the presence of

Jesus for His touch. To come to Him and listen to His voice, to cultivate our personal God time, to go back to the pain places so we can process through them, to stop coping and start healing, to open our hearts, to release and receive forgiveness, to repent for judgments and process memories, to see the emotional needs of our souls, to know what lies have taken root, and to grieve our losses.

We are called to a path of righteousness, a path of healing. One where peace is internal and external, where waters in our hearts that once were troubled are stilled, that we would dwell in not just a visitation of peace, but a habitation in quiet resting places.

> And the effect of righteousness will be peace [internal and external], and the result of righteousness will be quietness and confidence and trust forever. My people shall dwell in a peaceable habitation, in safe dwellings, and in quiet resting-places.
> —Isaiah 32:17-18 (AMPC)

Though my story has lots of traumas, it's easy to identify that I truly needed the healing touch of Jesus. The truth is, though, everyone needs the healing touch of Jesus. We all experience hurts, traumas, pain, and loss. Some that read this book may have a story like mine, others are radically different, but each is the same in that it is affected by the fall of man (see Genesis 1-3). Sin entered the world, and every single person is affected. Jesus promised us that we would have pain, sorrow, and trials.

"I have told you all this so that you may have peace in me. Here on earth you will have many trials and sorrows. But take heart, because I have overcome the world."

—John 16:33 (NLT)

We tend to minimize what we have been though. I hear comments such as:

- What I went through wasn't as bad as what she went through.

- What they went through was much worse than what I went through.

- I don't have it as bad as them, so it's not that bad.

- It's okay because God has a purpose.

- That was so long ago. God's still good.

All the while, their hearts are aching with an absence of peace. Jesus didn't say He came for the ones that had hard childhoods or the ones who have experienced significant traumas; He came for all humanity, that the world be saved.

> For God did not send His Son into the world to condemn the world, but that the world through Him might be saved.
>
> —John 3:17 (NKJV)

Remember, the word "saved" in Greek is *sozo*, meaning to make whole, deliver, heal, keep safe, to heal one suffering from disease, to save. Jesus came to give life abundant, to make humanity whole, to save us, deliver us, give us a safe place in Him, and heal those suffering from disease. He came to save.

We must press in and through what we've experienced. There are little "t" traumas and big "T" Traumas. And while there is truth that, when compared, some situations are much worse than others, if it caused you pain, it needs to be addressed so it can be healed.

If you're wondering if you need healing, I want to ask you this: Are there any situations or areas in your life or relationships that don't have the full manifestation of God's peace? I don't mean relationships where you are merely coping—I mean full peace. Any places in your life that don't have full rest or make it difficult for you to rest or be still?

We are in a broken world, a world where relationships can be complicated, and life can be hard. My heart is for you to welcome the Spirit of God into your heart where brokenness is (it could even be hiding), to let Him shine His light on those areas and bring full healing to you, body, soul, and spirit. The works of the enemy are to try to destroy all things good, to try to kill, steal, and rob from us and ultimately destroy us. Jesus came to destroy the works of the enemy.

> The thief comes only in order to steal and kill and destroy. I came that they may have *and* enjoy life, and have it in abundance [to the full, till it overflows]. I am the Good Shepherd. The Good Shepherd lays down His [own] life for the sheep.
> —John 10:10-11 (AMP)

> The reason the Son of God was revealed was to undo and destroy the works of the devil.
> —1 John 3:8b (TPT)

The wounds are in your heart, but just because they're buried or covered up doesn't mean they aren't still invoking pain and behaviors in your life today. The purpose in going back to go forward isn't to stir emotions or dig up old wounds. It is to go back to places that hold pain and invite Jesus into the emotions, places where hurt is and has been, to process with the One who can truly bring healing. Jehovah Rapha is the One who will mend, stitch, and heal our hearts. That is the purpose of going back is to heal so that we may go forward in the calling and purpose that God has on our lives.

The key to healing is being able to receive the love of God—not just a drop, but His endless embrace. When we make a choice to open our heart, that choices open a new door. We must push through the distraction and discomfort to fall into His embrace. When we move in closer to God, heaven will invade the brokenness and pain and will resurrect the joy that is our birthright.

> I am the Good Shepherd. The Good Shepherd risks *and* lays down His [own] life for the sheep.
> —John 10:11 (AMPC)

Jesus isn't just a good shepherd; He wants to be *your* shepherd. His gaze is upon you, and it's one of love and adoration. You can trust Him. Next to and in Him, we are safe. No matter where we are in life, His hand is always stretched out to us. He will lead us to a journey to get our hearts healed, and He will not abandon us. He will hold our hearts tenderly and remain because He can be trusted. His DNA is faithfulness and His loving kindness knows no end.

> . . . the true Shepherd of your lives—the kind Guardian who lovingly watches over your souls.
> —1 Peter 2:25b (TPT)

PROMPT:

If your heart is being stirred, I want to encourage you to pray this prayer:

> *Lord, I feel Your stirring in my heart. The Bible says that You are the kind Guardian that lovingly watches over my soul. I have areas in my heart and life that need Your touch. Jesus, I invite you to come and bring healing to every place where there is no peace. I welcome You into the process to bring healing into my heart and life, to make Your love known in new ways. I ask for healing in my body, heart, life, and relationships.*
>
> *In Your name, Jesus, amen.*

Be real with God in this moment. Speak out the areas where you need His touch, perhaps relationships that have conflict or areas that your finances need healing in—whatever you're feeling needs peace. If you suddenly have a memory pop up, bring that to Him. In this moment, tell Him what you're feeling and be honest in your prayers. He loves you and desires for you to walk in wholeness and healing. Don't just lay down this book, but take it back to the secret place in your God time. Allow God to help you tear down old structures of behaviors and thought patterns and replace them with His truth.

God's words bring healing to our hearts. I believe He will bring full healing and restoration to you.

Chapter Twenty

The Place

Several years ago in my God-Time, He gave me words that I penned "The Place."

I hope these words bless you.

THE PLACE

I AM the place the place you can escape to.
I AM the place where you're encircled with peace.
I AM the place where you're always seen.
I AM the place where you rest.
I AM the place where you are restored.
I AM the place where you are healed.
I AM the place where you are kept.
I AM the place where the floodwaters are stopped.
I AM the place where you can breathe.
I AM the place where you learn to have joy.
I AM the place where childhood is restored.
I AM the place where delight is felt like sunshine on your face.
I AM this place, dear one.

Remain here, in this place.

No matter where you are physically, let your heart and thoughts escape to the place where they are safe.

I AM the place of your refuge, healing, and delight.

This place is Me, dear one.

Thank you for reading my story.

> May the God of hope fill you with all joy and peace in believing [through the experience of your faith] that by the power of the Holy Spirit you will abound in hope and overflow with confidence in His promises.
> —Romans 15:13 (AMP)

About the Author

REBECCA COLEY IS A pastor, speaker, teacher, and author who writes from a deeply rooted Christian perspective to help others find inner healing and freedom in Christ.

With a compassionate heart and personal understanding of God's restoring power, she guides readers from trauma to wholeness. Teaching them how to release pain, connect intimately with God, and walk confidently in their divine calling. She has a remarkable testimony of resilience - overcoming impossible odds, surviving unimaginable trauma, and emerging healed, whole, and walking boldly in the calling of God in her life. She is known for her kindness, prophetic gifting, and her deep ability to hear the voice of God and help others learn to hear Him as well.

She founded Rebecca Coley Ministries. A ministry that reflects her passion to see lives transformed by the love and truth of Jesus. Whether speaking, writing, or ministering one-on-one, Rebecca's message remains the same: healing is possible, wholeness is real, and God still redeems every story.

— continued on next page —

She lives in North Carolina with her husband and remains deeply committed to a life marked by faith, excellence, and family. She finds peace and inspiration in the beauty of the outdoors.

Learn more at rebeccacoley.org and rebeccacoleyministries.org

www.ingramcontent.com/pod-product-compliance
Lightning Source LLC
LaVergne TN
LVHW020426070526
838199LV00004B/299